The GIFT IS YOU

❦

Encouragement for people seeking hope
during life's tough times

Remember you are special.
Your life can make a
difference.

Dr. David L. Wolf

with Connie Hurn

With Jesus there is Hope!

Dl Jow

www.xulonpress.com

For my wife, Anita,
my children,
Raquel and Brad,
and for those who are
searching for hope

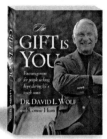

Praise for *The Gift Is You*

Because of David Wolf's wonderful book, *The Gift Is You*, I understand what I need in order to walk with Christ when my own body fails me. Lacking strength, I must rely upon the Lord. I related not only to Dr. Wolf's tragedy but also to his triumph, giving me renewed confidence in the victories that are possible only in Christ.

—**Frank Ball,** author of *Eyewitness: The Life of Christ Told in One Story*

Read this compelling, hard-to-put-down account of Dr. Wolf's circumstances only if you want to be inspired, humbled, and lifted up. With a deep love for God and a passion for God's people, Dr. Wolf writes about divine peace in the midst of tragedy. If you are discouraged and overwhelmed by the consequences of decisions you've made or things you've done, or if you enjoy helping others move through their challenges, this book is for you! Let the truths in this story transform your beliefs so you are encouraged. Then be the encouragement someone else needs.

—**Kathy Koch, PhD,** President and Founder of Celebrate Kids, Inc.

Dr. David Wolf's story shows the difference God's presence can make in anything life throws at us, whether the circumstances are of our own making or not. It can change your perspective on whatever you are facing, proving that no disaster needs to define us. God can use anything in your life if you are open to his transforming power.

—**Diane Eble,** author of *Abundant Gifts* (book and blog) and the Healing Heart Issues blog

A dramatic true story about a man many can identify with: a people-person with a passion to help others; a short-term missionary serving the poorest of the poor in Haiti; a go-kart racer who knows the adrenaline rush of the roar of the engine. But it is the Dr. David whose faith in God shines brightly when his whole world is changed forever that we come to know best in *The Gift Is You*. When the unthinkable happens and life is turned upside down, God walks us through to a complete recovery—physically, mentally, emotionally, and spiritually. When our legs will no longer carry us, the biggest "step" we can take is to turn all of our struggles over to God. He makes all the difference—and he is still able to use our gifts to glorify him. *The Gift Is You* is a triumphant story we all need to hear.

—**Elaine Wright Colvin,** Founder/Director of WIN India, WIN Communications, and Writers Information Network

Dr. Wolf shares his profound faith and his commitment to Jesus so that all who read this book can learn how to overcome the adversities we face in life. The strength he writes about is available to all if we are open to our Lord and Savior. Dr. Wolf's story offers us all hope. This is a must-read. Be prepared for a life-changing experience.

—**John E. Bodell, DO, OFS** (Secular Order of Franciscans), Associate Dean, Professor of Surgery, A. T. Still University, Kirksville College of Osteopathic Medicine

The power that drives David Wolf permeates every page of his writing. He is a man of many passions and strengths, and this story makes it uncompromisingly clear that they all stem from his love for God and his strength in Jesus Christ as his Savior. This book is not just an engaging read about the life experience of one man. This story draws you into a transparent revelation by a man who sees every difficult time as a process of discovering God's purposes. David wants his readers to catch the truth that God desires each of us to encourage others and make a lasting impact in this world. In our difficult times, we can shine a light on the paths of those who are struggling in the darkness. This is a must-read for anyone seeking hope and encouragement in God's provision for the hard times.

—**Jonathan Rohrer, PhD, DMin,** Associate Dean of Statewide Campus System, Michigan State University, College of Osteopathic Medicine

Dr. Wolf's remarkable journey in overcoming devastating physical injury to care for those less fortunate is a testament to the human spirit. Just as he's mentored numerous OB/GYN residents, Dr. Wolf teaches and inspires us about the healing power of faith. With a physician's discerning eye and a compassionate heart, Dr. Wolf examines the human condition with compelling observation and insight. This book is a prescription for how to find more meaning in life. Ultimately, that's Dr. Wolf's gift to us.

—**P. Charles Rossi, PhD,** marketing and communication consultant

Dr. Wolf's extraordinary personal warmth and his easygoing, articulate style make reading his prose a pleasure. Clearly, faith has carried him through experiences that would severely challenge anyone, and he shares his story in a humble, gentle manner that will benefit people who face tragedy and loss in their own lives. It is a heartfelt, uplifting memoir that eloquently tells a story of transcending grief. As Dr. Wolf's physician shortly after his injury, I watched this man undergo his rehabilitation, and it was more than inspiring. He used to cheer up the whole medical team on rounds, instead of vice versa. A rare man and a rare book.

—**Edward C. Nieshoff, MD,** Assistant Professor, Department of Physical Medicine and Rehabilitation, Wayne State University School of Medicine

As an osteopathic physician, I have worked with many disabled persons over the years. However, no one has made an impression on me as strong as David Wolf. Less than three months after David's life changed, he and his wife and his two children attended our biannual meeting in Chicago. When he described his accident and his daily routine to our group, you could have heard a pin drop on the thick carpet. Without a doubt, his courage had an impact on every person in that room. David's character is a true inspiration to everyone who knows him and anyone who reads about his experiences.

—**John S. Stevens Jr., DO,** board member, American Osteopathic Board of Obstetrics and Gynecology

Foreword

I first met Dr. David Wolf in the autumn of 1999. Shortly afterward, he asked me if I would like to visit his new OB/GYN clinic in downtown Trenton. I was amazed to find that he had built a beautiful chapel in his basement there. It was a wonderful experience to bow in prayer with this godly man as I began my ministry in the Downriver area of Detroit.

Two years later, David was in a tragic accident. One Sunday afternoon, I visited him in the hospital. He was surrounded by many loved ones and friends. I spoke to him quietly for a few minutes concerning the accident, then asked if I could pray for him.

"Pastor," he said, "there are some people around this bedside today who don't know Jesus and are not saved. I'd like you to pray for them first." Amazed at the quiet confidence displayed by this man of faith even at this time of life-changing crisis, I did as he asked me to do.

It has been my privilege since then to introduce Dr. Wolf to several congregational gatherings and to hear of his life's journey. He clearly sees what has happened to him as something that has opened up new vistas for service to his Lord. And because of his deep, abiding confidence in the providential care of the one true God revealed in and through his Son, Jesus Christ, David proclaims with the apostle Paul, "We know that in all things God works for the good of those who love him, who have been called according to his purpose" (Romans 8:28).

You too will come to know that all-embracing love of the Father God as you discover the great grace, mercy, and strength given to this man in his daily walk with Jesus.

Duane Armistead, DMin, retired pastor of the First Presbyterian Church of Trenton in Michigan

Acknowledgments

I started dreaming about writing this book in 2002. I never imagined the amount of time and critical thinking necessary to complete the project. After I'd been praying for two years, God sent me the perfect writing partner: Connie Hurn. Connie spent countless hours interviewing me and others who were a vital part of my life. She captured my heart and helped me write my story in the way God wanted it to be heard. I am forever grateful for her professionalism and unwavering commitment to this project. Most of all, I am thankful for the friendship we have developed through the years of working together.

My sincere thanks goes to Selah, a well-known gospel singing group. I've always listened to their music as a way of praying and praising God. Selah's award-winning song "Press On" became an important focus in my story.

Teamwork created the book you are holding now. My great thanks and appreciation goes out to many people for their contributions to this book:

Laurie Meadows, my office manager, for her support and daily encouragement.

Brad Sargent, editor, for his deep thought and creativity in editing the first draft of my manuscript.

Elaine Wright Colvin, Christian writing consultant, for her dedication to God and for making suggestions that enabled this book to appeal to a diverse range of readers.

Diane Eble, book publishing coach, for her sincere interest in *The Gift Is You* and expert advice given during many phone consultations.

Marisa Frazier, assistant, for hundreds of hours of typing and transcription services.

Linda Anderson, editor, for grammar, typing, and Bible research services.

Lauren Cleveland, marketing executive, for her vision, design, and development of *The Gift Is You* website, blog, and book promotion.

Annette LaPlaca, editor, for her proofreading services.

Richard Hurn, volunteer, for his proofreading services.

A special thank-you to Kathy Ide, my copyeditor and proofreader. Kathy required me to dig deep to answer questions readers would want to know. Her invaluable editing expertise has ensured that this book complies with literary excellence standards. Kathy's attention to detail, patience, and commitment to God's timing for this book made the final manuscript the best it could be.

I want to thank my family and friends for allowing themselves to be part of this book: my children, Brad Wolf and Raquel Haro; my sister, Sue Green; Dr. Paul Krueger, Frank Hajkus, Edie Sherman, Skip Bunton, Dr. Edward Nieshoff, Terri Little Loeckner, Dr. Robert Sauter, Dr. Raymond Deiter, and many others mentioned in the book.

I especially want to thank my pastor, Dr. Duane Armistead. He was always there for me and praying for me when I needed it most. He encouraged me to press on after my accident and provided the first speaking opportunities to share my testimony: "Press On" and "Your Life Can Make Difference."

My deepest gratitude goes to my wife, Anita, for being by my side since July 17, 1971. Her commitment to our wedding vows and constant support have made me a better person. Her godly suggestions and Bible verse cards placed discreetly on my desk will be remembered forever.

Finally, I want to give a heartfelt thanks to *The Gift Is You* prayer team. This group of faithful prayer warriors believes in the potential this book has for reaching people far and near. God bless you all.

Please visit **www.TheGiftIsYou.org** for a full list of prayer team members.

Proceeds from this book will be donated to:
- **Laban Ministries** (www.labanministries.org)
- **Northwest Haiti Christian Mission** (www.nwhcm.org)

Contents

Introduction

Life can try to steal your happiness and joy, especially when unexpected circumstances are thrown at you. Your future may seem
bleak. But it doesn't have to be.

Years ago, a tragic go-kart racing accident left me permanently
paralyzed. I could have given up or become bitter. Instead, God's
unbelievable presence sustained me. He helped me see that my situation
could be worse—I could have died! In time, he began using my
experiences to help other suffering people.

You may be thinking, *My hardship is worse than yours.* Or, *Mine
isn't as bad as yours.* Either way, there is hope. No matter what your
circumstances, God has a purpose for your life.

We all have dreams and fears, virtues and flaws. And we each have
a unique personality. But we don't all have a strong faith in God. Many
people believe in him, but only some actively put their faith in him,
especially during tough times.

Too often our confidence is determined by people, positions, posses-
sions, or misguided passions. Any of these can let us down and steer us
in the wrong direction, with outcomes that spell D-I-S-A-S-T-E-R!

There is only one thing we can count on consistently: God.

I'm a real man with real emotions—a barrel full of emotions that could
have destroyed me. Without God, my faith, and a personal relationship
with Jesus, my story would have a very different ending.

My tragedy did not break me, because my life is led by God, the giver
of the greatest gift of all: Jesus Christ. This is his gift to me and to you.

I am sharing my story because I believe it will reassure you and
provide hope when adversity strikes. Tragedy and trials have not limited
my life. The same can be true for you.

Each situation in this book demonstrates the truth of God's love and
grace, the power of prayer, and the blessing of encouragement provided
by others. I hope my story will inspire you and bring you closer to him.

My legs have been taken away, but nothing can stop me from walking with almighty God. Nothing can stop you, either.

"Which is easier: to say to the paralytic, 'Your sins are forgiven,' or to say, 'Get up, take your mat and walk'?" (Mark 2:9)

God bless you, dear friend.

Dr. David L. Wolf

1

Haiti Calls My Name

I want to wake up every day
and do something that matters.
NORMAN LEAR

On Saturday, January 30, 1999, Dr. Craig Hartman and I departed for a medical missionary trip to Haiti. It was less than twenty-four hours before the Super Bowl XXXIII kickoff.

Craig and I were eager to begin our adventure. He was one of my OB/GYN residents at Riverside Osteopathic Hospital, and this was our first time to join a mission team. During the flight we talked about our ambitious plans to work eighteen hours a day delivering babies and performing gynecological surgeries.

Being typical American sports fans, we automatically included Super Bowl Sunday in our conversation. We hated having to miss the game.

As it happened, the first leg of our American Airlines flight landed in Miami, host city for the Super Bowl. The Denver Broncos/Atlanta Falcons game promised to be great. Outstanding Broncos quarterback John Elway was retiring that year (after receiving the Most Valuable Player award). We would have enjoyed watching the game. No doubt about it!

The next leg of the flight took us from Miami to Port-au-Prince, Haiti's capital. Then we boarded a small, twenty-seat plane and waited several hours before taking off to Port-de-Paix, our last connecting flight to the mission. No explanation was given for the delay. The excitement of our adventure temporarily disappeared as we lived up to our impatient American reputation. We finally settled down when the flight took off.

As the plane descended I began questioning my decision to become a medical missionary in such a desolate place. The landing strip resembled something out of an Indiana Jones movie: a rocky dirt path with deep chuckholes. Though anxious to get off the plane, I wondered, *Are we really going to land here?* The answer: Yes!

Looking out the small window, I tensed up when we hit the rough turf. Dust flew, chickens scrambled, and people walked about, not bothered by the approaching plane. No one seemed concerned with getting out of harm's way. Some watched from behind a makeshift fence held together with thin wire and crooked wooden poles. Others tended to their business, carrying buckets of water or baskets of food on their heads. Most of the men, and even some women, were topless. *We definitely aren't in Kansas anymore!*

A pickup truck was waiting for us as we deplaned. Craig and I piled in the back with our gear. In a cloud of dust, we headed for the mission. Open ditches with raw sewage ran down the side of the dirt road. The stench turned my stomach.

This was "the real Haiti" I'd heard so much about.

During the bumpy, fifteen-mile drive, my mind drifted back to the first time I heard a conversation in the hospital where I worked about a medical mission project in Haiti. A surgery team from the Downriver Detroit area had gone there to help, and I was curious to learn about it.

For many years I'd managed an OB/GYN medical practice, delivering babies and performing surgeries at Riverside Osteopathic Hospital in Trenton, Michigan, in addition to working diligently with my OB/GYN residents. I had always thought about using my medical experience to help others less fortunate than I.

Eager to learn more, I talked with Dr. John Bodell, a good friend of mine who was in charge of the all-volunteer effort. He explained how his group supported the Northwest Haiti Christian Mission, located in Saint-Louis du Nord.

John painted a bleak picture of this primitive culture. "Haiti is a Caribbean island nation and one of the poorest countries in the Western hemisphere. Although only a few hundred miles separate the United States and Haiti, the Haitians are light years behind the US in their development. Most Haitians are illiterate and do not speak English. Almost one hundred percent of the Haitian people practice voodoo, the official religion of Haiti, yet they cherish receiving Bibles from America."

None of his discouraging description stifled my interest. "Tell me more."

"Haiti is a dangerous place," John continued, "due to great turmoil and political unrest. The citizens are governed by a dictatorship and are not accustomed to American freedoms. There are gangs and drug smuggling. Money coming into the country is often confiscated by government officials for their own use. The Haitians live in total poverty, and the lack of health care is a stark reality. Christian medical outreach provides an opportunity to meet their basic physical and spiritual needs simultaneously."

I asked what motivated him to go there.

"It's a wonderful opportunity to provide free health care for needy people and preach the gospel. I love helping people and making a difference—one person at a time."

That was exactly what I wanted to hear. My enthusiasm mirrored his. This was a mission I could throw my heart and soul into. "When is the next trip?"

He explained that surgery-team services were scheduled every year for seven days during the last week in January. Ophthalmology, dentistry, and other medical teams brought in by the mission served at different times of the year.

"I want to go with you next time."

He who is kind to the poor lends to the Lord, and he will reward him for what he has done. PROVERBS 19:17

Dr. Hartman also became interested in the mission trip after seeing a slide show presented by Dr. Bodell. He believed there was a genuine need for medical care in Haiti. Plus, he wanted the cultural experience.

We agreed to go together on the next trip. I was excited to be a part of this wonderful opportunity with such a great colleague.

We attended planning meetings on Sunday evenings at Dr. Bodell's home for about six months. Craig and I agreed to serve as part of the surgery team, but our focus was strictly on GYN surgeries and delivering babies.

This would allow me to meet three important personal objectives:

1. help less-fortunate people in need of OB/GYN medicine,
2. teach my residents about OB/GYN needs outside of the mainstream, and
3. introduce the Christian message to people who may never have another way to learn about Jesus Christ.

My greatest inspiration for going to Haiti was being able to share the belief and hope of Christianity with people in a poor, developing country.

Dr. Bodell handled all project logistics and helped with our mission applications. We were concerned about known diseases in Haiti. Immunizations for hepatitis A and B would be given before the trip, and medication to prevent malaria would be given before and after. I didn't want to take any chances with food and water, so I decided to pack my own bottled water and eat only granola bars for the seven days we were there.

Another big concern was OB/GYN medicines, supplies, and equipment. Dr. Bodell always relied on whatever was available at the mission, but we wanted to play it safe and decided to take our own scrubs, sutures, forceps, cord clamps, surgical instruments, and medications.

All the excitement and planning for this once-in-a-lifetime trip continued to run through my thoughts as we arrived at our final destination, Saint-Louis du Nord.

A French hospital occupied the original mission grounds. In 1979, the complex was purchased and converted to the Northwest Haiti Christian Mission by its founder, Pastor Larry Owen. Over time, the buildings were improved and other structures built to accommodate the growing needs of medical teams who came to help. The campus now included missionary housing, a school, an elder center, community center, and operation headquarters. The mission employed approximately ninety Haitians to help with housekeeping, cooking, indoor and outdoor maintenance, and interpreter responsibilities for visiting volunteers. Cement walls and iron fencing surrounded the mission. For security purposes, guards were stationed at the main gates twenty-four hours a day to minimize the risk of crime.

The moment we drove through the gated entrance, an undeniable sense of God's love and protection surrounded us. As my feet touched the ground, I knew this was a special place. Indescribable emotions washed over me, flooding my heart with peace and contentment. These feelings became embedded in my soul the entire time I spent in Haiti.

An unspoken unity pulsated through the mission community. Everyone shared the same beliefs and purpose. Knowing I could talk openly about God and pray with Haitian people anytime gave me a powerful sense of freedom. I could display my religious beliefs without worrying about hospital politics, my medical-practice overhead, or patients wanting to sue me.

Now the Lord is the Spirit, and where the Spirit of the Lord is, there is freedom. 2 CORINTHIANS 3:17

Craig and I unpacked our gear and set up a tent on the hard, bare ground. This would be our rugged living quarters for the next week. Then we walked to the surgery center. Although it was quite simple, all the essential elements were available. In the main area, we found adequate lighting, surgery and instrument tables, and portable IV stands. Metal racks, shelving, and plastic containers held all kinds of supplies, materials, and instruments. Additional tables lined the walls with miscellaneous items. I was pleasantly surprised.

Electricity was provided by diesel generators. The mission couldn't afford to run the generators twenty-four hours a day, resulting in the use of flashlights for nighttime emergencies. Craig and I had brought extra ones from home to be sure we would have enough light for our work at night. We'd done everything we could to be prepared, but I knew there would be a big learning curve.

When I was in the building, I felt filled with God's presence. The windows were made of clear glass blocks. Some had red stained-glass

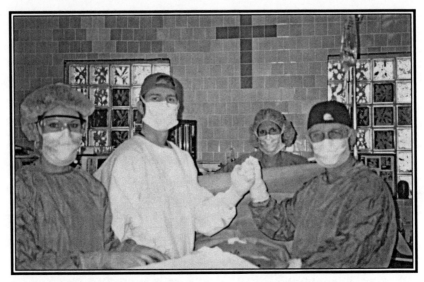

Ready to perform surgery in the operating room with my OB/GYN resident,
Dr. Craig Hartman, and the surgical team at the Northwest Haiti Christian Mission

crosses in the center. Sunlight streaming through the windows made the crosses stand out, a vibrant reminder of God's promise through Jesus Christ. Nondescript beige tiles covered the floor and walls—with one exception. An inlaid cross of dark blue ceramic tiles was centered on the wall where surgeries were performed, another cue of God's love and his living presence. The exterior of the building had stucco walls painted with scenes depicting stories from the Bible. There was a scene of Noah's ark and one of Jesus shepherding his flock—all beautiful signs of God's purpose for us in Haiti. The one I liked most was a Bible verse in Creole, painted on the wall next to the entrance: "He called a little child and had him stand among them. And he said: 'I tell you the truth, unless you change and become like little children, you will never enter the kingdom of heaven'" (Matthew 18:2–3).

Many Haitians waited hours or even days to receive health care. Free medical services set the stage for opening hearts and minds to God's Word. Our focus was based on the mission's purpose: "We exist to move people from where they are to where they should be—loving God and loving people."

I could hardly wait to see how God would use me to fulfill that lofty purpose.

2

Haiti's Surprise Blessing

When experience is viewed in a certain way, it presents
nothing but doorways into the domain of the soul.

JON KABAT-ZINN

D r. Hartman and I were humbled by the opportunities and challenges of the week ahead as we prepared our supplies and instruments for Monday's surgeries. Once those tasks were completed, we began daydreaming again about Super Bowl Sunday—the epitome of American tradition.

We came up with the bright idea of finding somebody with a TV so we could watch the game. One of our interpreters knew a well-to-do guy in the village. (There were only a few.) Extending his hospitality, the gentleman from the village invited us to his home to watch the Super Bowl. What more could we ask for? The game was scheduled to begin at six thirty.

The guy showed up on Sunday evening at almost dusk, about thirty minutes before kickoff, to drive us to his house. As we started to get into his truck, Mandella, one of the Haitian midwives, came running up to us and announced our help was needed to deliver a baby. The expectant mother was at home in a village among the foothills.

I looked at Dr. Hartman. Our eyes locked for a moment, each knowing the other's thoughts. *Work doesn't start until Monday morning!*

We had our first opportunity to do what we came here to do. But we really wanted to see the Super Bowl.

Our reason for coming to Haiti was crystal clear. How could we let the temptation of a football game—even the Super Bowl—get in the way of our purpose for being there?

"We've got a baby to deliver," I said to Craig. "Let's go!"

The only real hesitation was fear of the unknown. "What ifs" swirled in my head. What if something popped up that we weren't equipped to handle? I blocked out my skeptical thoughts.

Luckily we had spotted some empty buckets during our earlier walk through the surgery center. Craig and I had filled one of the buckets with the supplies needed for delivering a baby outside the mission: forceps, scissors, suture material and needle holder, cord clamp, local anesthesia with syringe, and sponges. I'd put it in my tent for safekeeping. I grabbed the bucket from my tent and forged ahead to the village, flashlight in hand.

Mandella guided us to the woman's small home. My heart pounded from the brisk trek up the mountainside. Mandella wasn't even breathing heavily.

Inside, we discovered the expectant mother had already delivered the baby on her own—a common practice in Haiti. She was lying on the dirt floor of the house, but the baby was not with her. My eyes darted around the dark, unfamiliar room and saw a naked infant lying on the ground, nestled in a pile of laundry a few feet away from the mother. (I later learned that Haitian mothers typically do not bond with their newborns until they are sure the babies will survive. Waiting two hours is standard.)

We delivered the placenta and re-clamped the baby's umbilical cord to prevent blood loss. Then we cleaned the newborn, wrapped her in a towel, and laid her beside the mother.

Mandella had done this job hundreds of times before. We were grateful she stepped back, allowing us to have this experience. She interpreted as I reassured both mother and father that the baby was okay. With folded hands and bowed head, I prayed quietly.

"Thank you, God, for performing the miracle of birth and for letting us take part in bringing a new life into this world. Please bless this family and show me how to bring them closer to you. In Jesus' name I pray. Amen."

Tears of joy flowed from everyone present.

> For the kingdom of God is not a matter of eating and drinking, but of righteousness, peace and joy in the Holy Spirit, because anyone who serves Christ in this way is pleasing to God and approved by men. ROMANS 14:17–18

After saying good-bye, Craig and I headed back to the mission feeling like we were on cloud nine. The dark night sky, blanketed with brilliant stars, reminded us that God was watching over all. I'm certain he was pleased with our decision to forego the Super Bowl. There would be more games to watch, but there would never be another birthing experience like our first one in Haiti. It left an indelible impression on my heart. Craig and I couldn't wait to begin our Monday surgeries.

> Remember this: Whoever sows sparingly will also reap sparingly, and whoever sows generously will also reap generously. Each man should give what he has decided in his heart to give, not reluctantly or under compulsion, for God loves a cheerful giver. And God is able to make all grace abound to you, so that in all things at all times, having all that you need, you will abound in every good work. As it is written: "He has scattered abroad his gifts to the poor; his righteousness endures forever." 2 CORINTHIANS 9:6–9

I awoke before dawn on Monday and took a cold shower. Then I went to the open-air patio at the far end of the dining pavilion and waited for the sun to come up. The solitude of daybreak prepared me for God's new day. I prayed and read my Bible. Watching the sunrise gave me a sense of God's presence and brought an exceptional closeness with him—something not easy to duplicate in my day-to-day workaholic lifestyle at home.

Haitian workers served breakfast in the dining area at six o'clock for the fifteen American volunteers. (I decided to stick with my bottled water and granola bars.) Devotional time was next, led by Pastor Owen. He read Bible verses that focused on building God's kingdom. The verses included the importance of using our gifts to serve and glorify God. Hymns in English would end our devotional time. I liked this well-organized morning routine.

Before departing for the surgery center, Pastor Owen announced that we should finish our workday by five o'clock and that dinner would be served at six. His greatest emphasis was on the seven o'clock evening devotionals, which he expected the missionaries to provide. It was his way of encouraging our spiritual development.

A sign-up sheet was distributed. I signed up for the last night. I figured that would give me a week's worth of experiences to think about and choose the most meaningful things to share.

> **Let the word of Christ dwell in you richly as you teach and admonish one another with all wisdom, and as you sing psalms, hymns and spiritual songs with gratitude in your hearts to God. And whatever you do, whether in word or deed, do it all in the name of the Lord Jesus, giving thanks to God the Father through him.** COLOSSIANS 3:16–17

Surgeries were scheduled to begin at eight. Our assignments were written on a piece of paper given to us by one of the mission's administrative workers. Craig and I performed ten tubal ligations and three deliveries our first day.

One of the workers came into the operating room as we were finishing our last surgery of the day and announced that there was someone outside who wanted to see me. (Luckily, we were not in the middle of a surgery.) I couldn't imagine what was going on, so I took an interpreter with me. A man and woman stood in the surgery waiting room, holding a newborn. I didn't recognize them.

"Thank you for delivering our baby last night," the man said through the interpreter. "We are the Odelus family, and we want you to name our baby."

I was stunned by their request. Yet a joy-filled memory of the previous night flooded my heart with gratitude. I realized that I hadn't recognized the couple at first because the delivery scene had been lit only by a flashlight.

"Thank you," I replied. "This is an honor. But I don't know any Haitian names."

"It doesn't matter," said the father.

The first name that came to my mind was my wife's. But Anita was difficult for them to pronounce. So I suggested her middle name, Sue.

Both father and mother smiled and nodded with approval. "Sue. Sue. Sue," they repeated over and over.

The father spoke again through the interpreter. "We are blessed by your devotion to the mission and your willingness to come to our home in the night. Will you be our baby's godfather?"

"Yes," I said humbly, with tears in my eyes. "I would be honored to be your baby's godfather." But I wondered why they wanted to bestow this honor on me. I hadn't done anything spectacular. *I'm a doctor who delivers babies. I just did my job.* To this day, I call her "Baby Sue" and continue serving as her godfather. I pray for the family and stay in touch by writing letters with words of encouragement and the hope found in Jesus.

Let another praise you, and not your own mouth; someone else, and not your own lips. PROVERBS 27:2

Every day in Haiti, I reflected on my experiences and planned for the last day's devotions. I decided my message would focus on the unexpected gifts I'd received, such as helping with Baby Sue's birth and the honor of being her godfather.

When my turn came to speak, I acknowledged all of the medical missionaries for their commitment to Haiti as they served with no thought of getting something in return. I exclaimed over God's undeniable presence throughout the mission and the beautiful atmosphere of spiritual giving. Most important, I let them know that even though we each had our own reason for being there, God's purpose was much greater. He wanted us to express his love by bringing people to Jesus. That was the fruit of our labor.

Our God is awesome! He pours his gifts into the hearts of his disciples—gifts of peace, joy, and intimacy with Jesus.

Blessed are those who hunger and thirst for righteousness, for they will be filled. MATTHEW 5:6

Leaving Haiti at the end of the week was bittersweet. I was sad to leave the mission, where everyone shared a special sense of God's love and an opportunity to serve him through the gifts of medicine and Christianity. But during our return flight, my excitement for telling people back home about my experiences outweighed my sadness over leaving. In between dozing off and on, Dr. Hartman and I talked with anticipation and certainty of our plans for returning to Haiti the next year.

Baby Sue (age 8) and her father outside the surgery center at the Northwest Haiti Christian Mission

3

Haiti Leaves an Indelible Mark

Only that day dawns to which we are awake.
HENRY DAVID THOREAU

The following year, my second trip brought more rewarding experiences with the opening of the Tender Lambs Birthing Center. It was a dream come true for Dr. Ross Duff, an American OB/GYN who was instrumental in its development. The center provided a controlled setting with birthing rooms. As a result, approximately six hundred deliveries were performed that year, compared to two hundred the year before.

Craig went with me again. We were in our glory!

Having heard my Baby Sue story, many members of the new surgery team were eager to visit her family. Most of the team brought clothes and other gifts for Sue and her family.

When Saintano Odelus, Baby Sue's father, heard I was in Haiti again, he showed up at the birthing center and invited the surgery team to his home.

To avoid interrupting the surgery schedule, we decided to visit on Friday after surgery shut down. It would be our last day at the mission before heading back to the States and a great way to end our adventure.

After cleaning up on Friday, twelve members of the team gathered in the dining room at five o'clock. It was still daylight. An interpreter met us there to lead the way.

We spent an hour walking the mountainside footpaths to the Odelus home. Many of them were merely dried-up, rocky creek beds. We had to maneuver around broken tree limbs, scruffy brush, and jagged rocks. We held hands through several stages of the obstacle course.

The Odelus home resembled many others in Haiti: a small, flimsily built, four-walled cement structure with window and door openings that allowed air and light to enter. There were no glass panes or wooden doors, only blankets, sheets, or shutters over the openings for privacy. Roofs were either thatched or made from plywood scraps or corrugated metal. Quite a contrast to my Trenton, Michigan, home. And yet these modest people took as much pride in their houses as we do. The Odelus home had clean walls, a front yard of raked dirt and trimmed shrubbery, and no trash anywhere.

We were greeted like honored guests: with welcoming smiles, handshakes, and Sunday-best clothes. Mrs. Odelus wore a cotton floral dress. Mr. Odelus wore slacks and a colorful short-sleeved shirt. Their six children were dressed in bright outfits as well. And their shoes were shined. Baby Sue had a pink bow clipped to her hair.

"Please come in," said Mr. Odelus through the interpreter. The space was small, so Dr. Hartman and I and four others entered while the rest waited outside.

A tapestry with Jesus shepherding a flock of lambs was tacked on the wall in front of us. It served as a backdrop to a white-linen-covered table, where a cake decorated with pink and yellow icing was displayed. I could hardly believe they'd made us one! It looked as good as any homemade dessert I'd seen in the States. Next to it was a container of locally made liqueur.

I took the wonderful treats outside for the others to admire. Mrs. Odelus offered them to everyone as a gesture of love and appreciation.

With the aid of our interpreter, I served as spokesman for the group. "Thank you for your kind welcome and generosity. You have made us feel very special."

"We are grateful you helped with the birth of our baby and for naming her," the father said. "We are honored you are her godfather."

"The mission has made a difference for many people we know," the mother said as tears welled up in her eyes. "I love learning about Jesus, and I treasure my Bible. Thank you."

My eyes misted as I gave a heartfelt prayer. "Dear Lord, thank you for the Odelus family's hospitality today. We are grateful for the food, the fellowship, and especially the blessings you have given us through this Haitian family. Please let them continue to have everlasting hope in Jesus Christ, and help all of us here remember to trust you in all circumstances, today and tomorrow. Amen."

After everyone enjoyed the delicious cake and liqueur, two of our nurses presented gifts to each family member. Wrapping paper and ribbon flew as packages were eagerly unwrapped. The children squealed with delight. Thank-yous echoed from every child.

I handed Mr. Odelus an envelope containing five hundred dollars. He was speechless.

When the celebration concluded, several of us helped clean up dishes and dispose of trash. Many hugs and handshakes were given as we said our good-byes and headed back to the mission.

Heart connections had been made. The team now had a sense of my personal experience with the Odelus family. Every person who trekked up the mountainside, gift in tow, now had his or her own memories to share.

On the return flight to the US, I heard chatter from tired team members who were making plans to tell their stories. I hoped they would inspire others to join us in Haiti on the next trip.

In 2001, I looked forward to returning to Haiti more than anything else that year. Dr. Hartman planned on going with me a third time. Working at the Tender Lambs Birthing Center was a perfect way for me to serve the Lord. It allowed me to combine the things I love the most: serving God, performing deliveries and surgeries, and working with a great resident.

My third visit was extra special because Anita joined our mission team. Her experience as a nurse was a great asset. More important, her love of the Lord was in perfect harmony with the mission's purpose.

Baby Sue was uppermost on my mind when I arrived. I couldn't wait to see how she had grown. Team members took clothing for the family again. Giving money seemed practical, but I discovered it wasn't prudent. Word had gotten back to me that the money given the second year had been taken by government officials for their own use. I wanted to give something more meaningful this time.

Anita and I decided to purchase a gift for the Odelus family that would keep on giving—two pigs, a male and a female. The parents could mate the pigs, keep some of the piglets for themselves, and sell others to help with additional family needs.

Getting the pigs up the mountain would require creativity, determination, and a sense of humor. We couldn't drive them in a vehicle, because there was no road. And they were heavy and impossible to carry. So Craig and I put homemade leashes on them.

After wrestling to get the leashes on the pigs, we headed up the mountain, already exhausted. Getting those stubborn animals to walk with us was a feat of strength, endurance, and patience. If my colleagues back in Michigan could have seen me, they would have laughed. But at the time, it was no joke to me!

We were sweaty and dusty when we arrived at the Odelus home. But I was excited to present the unique gift. The Odeluses came out into the yard when they heard the snorting pigs. They seemed surprised. "Thank you," said Mr. Odelus with raised eyebrows. But that was the only response, other than subtle smiles when the children began petting the pigs.

Unfortunately, the pigs were not used the way I anticipated. The father sold both of them right away. I was greatly disappointed. But I could not control the choice made by the recipient of my gift.

At the end of my third visit, I left even more of my heart in Haiti and came home with a greater desire to return. Craig and I began dreaming about putting together our own OB/GYN team for helping the mission.

But my medical practice and the business of health care consumed my attention, leaving little time for anything else.

4

The Prayer of Jabez

We have to pray with our eyes on God, not on our difficulties.
Oswald Chambers

My practice grew steadily until 2001, when the health-care industry started drastically changing. The cost of malpractice insurance skyrocketed, insurance companies were gaining more control of patient-care choices and reimbursement decisions, and employee wages and benefits increased. All of these factors painted a discouraging picture for continued success.

In April, Anita and I met with our accountant and tax attorney for the annual review of my medical practice. We were told our expenses exceeded our revenue. The recommendation was to lay off my highest-paid staff. I didn't like that idea one bit.

"What are we going to do?" Anita asked during the sober ride home.

"I think we should pray," I said. "I'm going to start praying the prayer of Jabez. That's the best thing to do."

> Oh, that You would bless me indeed, and enlarge my territory, that Your hand would be with me, and that You would keep me from evil, that I may not cause pain!
>
> 1 Chronicles 4:10 NKJV

I had discovered this prayer, and a discussion of its meaning and implications, in a powerful book called *The Prayer of Jabez* by Bruce Wilkinson.[1]

As I began surrendering to God the financial dilemma facing my medical practice, I needed a deeper kind of prayer. And this one seemed the perfect answer.

I prayed faithfully every day. "Dear Lord, bless my practice and me. Help me to understand and discern what you want. Please guide me so I won't hurt anyone. And please, Lord, open my horizons to serve you better. In Jesus' name I pray. Amen."

I put my whole heart into that prayer. It gave me peace and helped me release my problems to God.

> **Endure hardship as discipline; God is treating you as sons.**
> **For what son is not disciplined by his father?** HEBREWS 12:7

I kept seeing patients during this time of uncertainty. One of my greatest joys was sharing my faith when troubled patients opened up to me.

"As long as I have God and my family, I could sweep the streets of Trenton for a living and be happy." I'd made this statement with conviction hundreds of times through the years. I wanted my patients to turn to God for help during their challenges and hardships.

Now that I was facing challenges myself, this statement took on new meaning. For some reason, the wording changed slightly after I received the bad news at our annual meeting. "As long as I have God and my family, I could be paralyzed and sweep the streets of Trenton for a living and still be happy."

I don't know what made me start saying it that way. At the time, I had no way of knowing what was in store for my future. But I don't think my words were a coincidence. God, in his grace and mercy, was preparing me for a life I couldn't imagine.

5

Racing Go-Karts
Was in My Blood

It is with our passions as it is with fire and water;
they are good servants, but bad masters.

ROGER L'ESTRANGE

July 29, 2001, dawned with clear blue skies and an expected high of 90 degrees in Trenton, Michigan. With very little wind, it was a perfect Sunday for my passionate hobby: adult go-kart racing.

I'd loved racing since I was a boy, when my Uncle Orla introduced me to the Indianapolis 500. As spectators we watched with excitement. It became an annual tradition for me to attend the races with him.

Uncle Orla and Aunt Opal couldn't have children of their own, so I was like a son to them. My family spent a lot of time at their home in Sharpsville, Indiana, fifteen miles from our home in Kokomo.

When I was in sixth grade, Uncle Orla asked me, "Would you like to watch some go-kart racing?"

"Sure!"

The first time we went to a race, the high-pitched roar of screeching engines grabbed my attention. The loud noise excited me as I watched go-karts speed around the track. Each driver had an intense look in his eyes. The competition was fierce. Everyone wanted to win. Their competitive spirit mesmerized me.

I soon started talking about getting a go-kart myself and racing with the other kids. I only saw one problem. The races were held in a farmer's field on a dirt track, and I didn't like the idea of having a dirty go-kart.

When my uncle took me to a race on a paved track, my interest reignited. I started bugging my dad for a go-kart. He finally indulged my one-track mind and bought me one. For the rest of sixth grade, and through seventh and eighth grades, I participated in races. Every one was exciting. Go-kart racing was in my blood.

As I grew into manhood, go-kart racing faded to a boyhood memory as I became consumed with the goal of becoming a physician.

During her appointments with me, one of my patients, Alicia, started talking to me about go-kart racing. Her father, Danny Doyle, was a go-kart mechanic.

When she came in for her six-week checkup, Alicia said, "My dad wants to know if you'd like some tickets to watch a go-kart race in Toledo."

I chuckled. "If I go to a go-kart race, I won't be watching it. I'll be racing in it!"

Two hours later Danny called. "I hear you'd like to race."

I told him I'd been kidding about that.

"Do you prefer an oval or a road course? Asphalt or dirt?"

"Now, hold on a minute. I don't have time for go-karts. The races are on Sundays, and I do deliveries on the weekend."

"Doc, you work 24/7. You need to have some fun! I'll fax you the schedule. Then we'll talk again."

I decided to give it a try and told my residents what I planned to do. They cheered me on. But I didn't know if I really had the guts and skill at age fifty-four to win an adult go-kart race. I didn't want to lose and be embarrassed to tell my residents.

The first day at the Toledo Speedway brought back vivid memories of winning go-kart races as a kid. The sights and sounds were the same, with only one difference. These were men, not boys!

I borrowed Danny's equipment and one of his karts. My adrenaline and competitive spirit kicked in on my first race. And I won! That was the beginning of three exciting years of go-kart racing.

Cost issues concerned Anita. "Go-kart racing is an expensive sport," she said. "I don't think you should be using our household income for it."

Her point was well taken.

Since the beginning of my medical career I'd provided continuing medical education at least once a year for physicians through financial incentives from the pharmaceutical companies. So I contacted Eli Lilly Pharmaceuticals and asked if I could give extra lectures three or four times a year. The additional income covered the cost of my go-kart passion. I loved lecturing and traveling to various medical conferences locally and out of state. And Anita was happy to let me go by myself because her work schedule and volunteer commitments kept her very busy. My partners and I covered for one another on numerous occasions, so handling my patients wasn't a problem either.

Thanks to my added income from Eli Lilly, I was able to hire two go-kart mechanics. I also indulged in having two engines, just in case one blew up, and two kart bodies, in case one got wrecked in a crash. This way I wouldn't have to miss a single race due to waiting for repairs.

The second year, Anita finally watched me race once. That's all it took for her to be convinced of the dangers.

After the race, in the privacy of our home, she pleaded, "David, please stop racing. This is a young person's sport, and you're not a kid anymore." The frightened look in my wife's eyes made her wishes clear.

The risks of adult go-kart racing made me nervous too. But competition flowed through my body, a constant companion every time I raced. I couldn't give it up.

My son, Brad, and my daughter, Raquel, also urged me to give up racing. I ignored their concerns as well. Nothing could stop my intense, goal-oriented personality—and my need to prove I was not getting old.

The first and second years, I won races about 70 percent of the time. The third year started out the same. I envisioned July 29 at the Toledo Speedway to be a winning day for me as well. I woke up early—no alarm clock needed. When Anita awakened, I asked, "Are you sure you don't want to go to the race track with me today?"

"Absolutely not!" Her position on the subject had remained the same since the one time she watched me race.

To make matters worse, I'd flipped my kart the week before and fractured two ribs. I didn't go to the hospital, and I didn't make a big deal about it. In spite of the risks, I was determined to continue racing. But the incident was fresh in Anita's mind.

I went out to get the Sunday paper and took in a deep breath of fresh air to help control my nerves. The pain of bending down to pick up the paper off the driveway reminded me of Anita's legitimate concerns. I prayed for safety.

My Sunday morning ritual was to leisurely read the paper, sipping hazelnut coffee, then get ready for church. After attending the eleven a.m. service with Anita, we'd go out for brunch. I loved having one day a week in my fast-paced, workaholic life when I didn't have to hurry.

But races were scheduled to start at one o'clock in the summer, which meant either skipping church or attending the eight o'clock service. Anita made it clear that she would not get up that early on Sunday. So we decided to attend separately.

Giving up our only focused time together was a big disappointment for both of us. Other than those few hours a week, we seldom spent much time together, except for an occasional vacation. Anita never complained. She knew racing was important to me, and she figured it wasn't worth an argument.

Summer Sundays were scheduled around my getting to the Speedway on time for the first race. I even arranged for my Sunday baby deliveries to be performed by my associates. It was a big sacrifice for Dr. Ahmad Al-Jerdi and Dr. Arleigh Ancheta. But they understood that nothing would deter me from my racing passion.

When I returned home from church that morning, I quickly changed from my suit and tie into my race-day uniform: cut-off jeans, a green scrub shirt, and my favorite well-worn moccasins. *Ah, total comfort.*

I packed some peanut-butter sandwiches, bottled water, and a Coke in my travel cooler, then took off for the races.

Normally, I drove Anita's SUV to Toledo because I didn't want to get my Lincoln dirty. But Brad had the SUV at the lake. If I drove the Lincoln, Anita would not have a way to get to church. But she agreed to accommodate my needs by skipping church. She didn't have any other plans that day.

Anyone who knows me understands I take great pride in my vehicles. I've been this way since my youth, when I convinced my dad to buy me my first car—a pink 1957 Thunderbird. Yes, pink. It was used, but it was awesome! I was only fifteen and too young to get a driver's license. But I washed or polished it every day—spring, summer, and fall—until the first snow. I finally got my license when I turned sixteen. But I refused to drive that car in the rain or to school because I didn't want it to get dirty.

When I was about to start college, I bought a 1949 Plymouth. My uncle fixed it up at his paint-and-body shop. I drove that to school while my T-bird stayed in my parents' garage. I still washed it every day I could until I sold it in 1982.

My buddy Frank Haikus usually drove with me to the track. Frank didn't race, but he was the only one in my circle of family and friends who shared my passion for the sport. He was an enthusiastic spectator and my personal sideline coach.

That Sunday Frank decided not to join me. I was participating in a "no-points race," which meant it didn't count toward the championship. Besides, the weather was hot, which wouldn't be much fun for him. Though I'd miss my "cheerleader," I didn't mind having the drive all to myself. It gave me time to mentally prepare for the race.

I called my sister, Sue, during my drive to Toledo, to catch up on family news.

"I can't believe you're going back there after fracturing two ribs," she scolded. "You were lucky last week. You may not be so lucky the next time. What are you trying to do, kill yourself?"

My big sister, two years older than I am, was just trying to look out for me. But she should've known a couple of fractured ribs weren't going to stop me from racing.

"You don't need to worry about me. I can handle it."

After we hung up my mind reverted to thinking about the new alcohol engine that had been installed by my mechanics, Danny Doyle and Bill Litigot. I paid them to keep my go-kart in tip-top shape. I hoped they had everything ready for me to compete in the alcohol-racing division. It was my decision to enter this new-to-me category, but I wondered how well I'd be able to compete against experienced alcohol-engine racers.

Could I handle the faster speed and still control my go-kart? How would the other drivers treat me? Would they be mad that I'd jumped racing divisions? Would they try to cut me off? Did I have the talent and skill necessary to win?

The questions kept me motivated—and anxious. The results of this race would determine whether or not I'd be able to enter the four-man, five-hundred-lap Alcohol Endurance Race coming up in two weeks—a race I definitely wanted to win!

6

Thrill of the Race

To win you have to risk loss.
JEAN-CLAUDE KILLY

When I arrived at the Toledo Speedway, a rush of adrenaline pumped through my body before my feet touched the ground. Spectators overflowed the stands. Go-karts were being rolled off their trailers and pushed to the pits. Drivers made final checks of their karts. Most of them didn't have special mechanics like I did.

When I got to my slot, I asked Danny and Bill the usual questions.

"How's the oil?

"What about the spark plug? Did you install a new one this week?"

"How's the air pressure in the tires? Are we using the same ones for this race as we did for slower speeds?"

Their answers were important because my eighteen-hour workday schedule didn't give me a chance for a test drive.

"Did you test the new engine?"

"How fast did it go?"

"How well did it take the turns?"

My apprehension was apparent, but I was focused on winning. And I had everything I needed: two great mechanics, a perfect go-kart, phenomenal adrenaline, a highly competitive spirit, and an unbelievable desire to win.

"Danny," I asked, "do you think I stand a chance in the alcohol division?"

I wanted him to say, "Yes, absolutely." But I knew he'd give me an honest answer.

"You know, Doc, you may not be able to win this time. You've never competed at this level before, and these guys have been racing the faster engines for a long time. It's going to take a while for you to adjust." He grinned. "Then again, I'm not sure if you can handle not winning."

Danny knew I had to win to be happy. I didn't want to spend three or four years getting up to par with the other racers. Yet his remarks got my attention. "Well, I'm going to stay focused. There's no way I'm going to lose this one!"

I headed to the locker room to change into my thousand-dollar, custom-made racing outfit. My suit, gloves, helmet, racing collar, and shoes all matched—in Notre Dame Blue. I'd always loved Notre Dame because they have a tradition of excellence and winning. The colors reminded me of their greatness—something I wanted to duplicate.

My go-kart was even painted Notre Dame Blue, with gold flames and a gold number 7. Seven was Brad's hockey number; choosing it was my way of showing pride in my son's athletic ability.

I completed my pre-race ritual by waxing a winning shine on my kart.

I was ready to race. Ready to win.

The eleven other racers and I drew numbers from a hat for first-heat race positions. I drew #12. My shoulders slumped in disappointment.

The kart in position #1 made a parade lap, controlling the other karts' speed until the green flag was given to start the race.

Despite the disadvantage, I finished fourth in the first heat. Not bad. That gave me a better starting position for the second heat.

This time I was in position #3. I only had to beat the first and second karts.

I put on my racing collar and helmet, securing the strap under my chin. Snug gloves went on last.

I was one inch from the ground. Seatbelts were not permitted because it is safer to be thrown out of a go-kart if an accident occurs.

"Gentlemen, start your engines!"

Every engine roared to life at the same time. The thrilling sound gave me a huge surge of adrenaline.

In the winner's circle after a race at the Toledo Speedway

The starter held up two fingers and the two parade laps began.

As the second lap neared its final turn, I prepared to floor my gas pedal. My front tires were almost touching the back tires of the guy in the pole position. *If I get any closer, I'll roll over him.*

As we approached turn four, the starter held the green flag high. Finally, the pole-position kart's tires crossed the line.

Heart pounding, I jammed my foot to the floor and quickly reached sixty miles per hour, staying almost on top of the kart in front of me.

The first turn came up fast. The first and second karts started spinning, forcing me to make a split-second decision. If I ran into them, I'd risk their lives, wreck my kart, and not win!

I turned the wheel hard to the right, trying to pass them on the outside of the track. A dangerous move, but I managed to miss them.

I put a death grip on the steering wheel as my reflexes forced the wheel hard left. Without warning, I swerved, slamming my back tires into the concrete retaining wall.

The next thing I remember is being on my back, semiconscious, on the ground. I felt no pain, but I kept saying, "I can't breathe! I can't breathe!"

7

His Voice

*Don't wait until you have
a tragedy to get strong.*
JOYCE MEYERS

Hold on, Dr. Wolf, we're almost there. You can make it."
I heard the medical technician's voice through a mental fog.

The Toledo Speedway had an ambulance at the track for every race. I had chatted with the friendly driver before I raced.

"We've called ahead to Saint Vincent's Hospital, alerting the ER trauma team to be ready."

As soon as we arrived at the emergency entrance, I was taken out of the ambulance and rushed to a trauma room. I passed out and became unconscious before any further action took place.

Anita was doing laundry when the phone rang.

"Anita, it's Connie." Anita had met the wife of Premier Karting Association owner Kevin Greer before. "Kevin asked me to call you," Connie said calmly. "Your husband was involved in an accident today. He's being taken to Saint Vincent's Hospital in Toledo. They want to hold him for observation in the ER until you can get there."

Anita was concerned but not shocked. She pictured me just banged up a bit, assuming this incident was similar to my fractured ribs two weeks earlier. "I'll be there as soon as possible."

Moments later she realized she didn't have a vehicle. After making a few phone calls, she finally reached Dr. Robert Sauter, an anesthesiologist who was also a friend.

"I'll be there right away," he said.

Bob didn't show up for several minutes, which didn't surprise Anita. He'd always been a laid-back kind of person.

While Anita was waiting for Bob, Connie phoned again, asking if she was coming. The second call made Anita wonder if this was more of an emergency than she originally thought. She assured Connie she would be on her way as soon as her ride came.

When Anita finally arrived at the hospital, she saw my mechanic, Danny, in the waiting room. He sat in a plastic chair, my racing uniform lying across his lap, cut cleanly down the middle. In one hand Danny held my wedding ring.

Anita gasped.

Danny looked up when he heard her. Without a word, he handed Anita my personal belongings. His silence told her something was seriously wrong.

Anita and Bob followed a nurse to the trauma room. She found me on a respirator, heavily sedated, and apparently unconscious. Emergency Department trauma physician Dr. Rachael Navakovic and the hospital chaplain were waiting for them.

Anita appreciated having the chaplain available for support, but she was not prepared for Dr. Navakovic's stoic announcement.

"Dr. Wolf cannot move his legs. Ten ribs are completely fractured, eight on the left and two on the right. And all of the spinous processes in his back are broken." Spinous processes are the little bumps you can feel on your backbone. "He is being transported to Neurology Intensive Care. After further evaluation the neurosurgeon will give you his report."

Anita's face flushed, and her stomach knotted up. She was speechless. But she was grateful to God for sending Bob to be with her in this moment of crisis. His easygoing personality, medical knowledge, and experience with challenging patient situations gave him the perfect qualifications to help her hear the bad news and make decisions about important next steps.

Though bewildered by this crisis, Anita knew that family members, close friends, and office staff needed to be notified of the serious accident. She went through the motions of making phone calls on automatic pilot.

That evening, Brad, Raquel, and Sue arrived at the hospital. They huddled together in the Neuro ICU family waiting room, fearing the report from the neurosurgeon.

Dr. McCormick did not have good news. "David's spine has been completely severed. I expect he will be paralyzed from the waist down for the rest of his life."

Raquel fainted. A nurse came immediately to assist her.

Brad punched the door and walked out of the room. "Why did he throw his life away on something he could have prevented? He should have listened to Mom's advice and given up his need for go-kart racing."

Sue, exhausted from her five-hour drive, wrapped her arms around Anita and sobbed. After regaining some composure, her tears still flowed, but she gathered enough strength to help Anita make phone calls to update loved ones on my condition.

Anita appreciated her sister-in-law's support, but the devastating shock remained. There was so much to learn, think through, and decide.

Just minutes before the start of Sunday evening Bible study at First Presbyterian Evangelical Church of Trenton, Anita called the pastor, Duane Armistead, and asked the church to pray.

"I'll have the elders take over," he told Anita, "and I'll be down there as soon as I can."

Pastor Armistead was new to the church. He didn't know us well, yet he felt compelled to be with our family. His immediate change of plans to be at our side and his obvious compassion, even before knowing how serious the accident was, began a deep friendship.

For the next two days, I lay in a Neuro ICU bed with my eyes closed, under heavy sedation. During that time, an unbelievable tranquility came over me.

God spoke to my spirit. "I am with you and the ones you love. I will encourage you and strengthen you to press on. I will carry you when you can't walk and pick you up when you are weak. I love you and have a new mission for your life."

His voice was soothing. It gave me hope. His presence surrounded me. His love radiated through my broken body.

May your unfailing love rest upon us, O Lord, even as we put our hope in you. PSALM 33:22

I thought of Haiti and everything I still wanted to do there. Yet I didn't dwell on the past and get swallowed up in the quicksand of self-pity. Instead, my faith grew stronger. God had blessed me with memorable experiences in Haiti. I needed to trust him to provide more such blessings.

I knew this was the beginning of a deeper and more personal relationship with him, stronger than I had ever experienced. I was being prepared by sovereign God for work yet to be done, and I felt enormously blessed.

My eyes remained closed. I was barely surviving on a respirator and IVs. Yet in my heart I felt the complete assurance of God's love.

I felt total peace just listening to his voice.

Jesus said, "He who has ears to hear, let him hear." MARK 4:9

After two days in Neuro ICU, my sedation was lessened and my eyes finally opened. As I regained consciousness, I saw Anita, with my wedding ring dangling from a gold chain around her neck. My mind flooded with emotion and memories as I gazed at her tear-filled eyes.

I mumbled something incoherent. Anita found a tablet and pen, and gave them to me. With shaking hands, I scratched out a note, but it was impossible to read.

I'm a doctor, I thought. *I'm supposed to have poor handwriting.*

I kept trying until my scribbling became legible. Knowing marriages can easily fall apart when crisis strikes a family, I wrote, "Don't forget your wedding vows."

Wedding photo of Anita and me before leaving the church, July 17, 1971

Anita reassured me with a hug. No words were necessary.

Over the next two days, my notes became easier to decipher. Pen glued to my hand and well supplied with paper, I wrote constantly. My mind wouldn't shut off. I was determined to be heard.

Two days passed before Dr. McCormick gave orders for me to be taken off the respirator. That day he met with my family privately to prepare them for my prognosis. Afterward, Anita, Brad, Raquel, and Sue came to my room and prayerfully watched as the breathing apparatus was removed.

I had survived the critical zone of dying. But I still couldn't move my legs or sit up. Multiple IV lines and tubes were connected to many parts of my body. But being able to breathe on my own was a great relief.

The nurse helped me get as comfortable as possible before calling Dr. McCormick into the room. Anita stood by the bedside and took my hand. Her face paled when he arrived. I braced myself for his news.

"David," he said, "you are paralyzed from the waist down. And this is going to be a permanent condition. You need surgery on your spine to prevent further damage. We'll have to graft in bone and insert two titanium rods on either side of your vertebrae. Moving you would be risky, but I recommend you go to the University of Michigan Hospital for the procedure. That hospital is recognized for their success with this type of situation."

"Looks like I have some new challenges ahead of me," I said calmly. Everyone in the room stared at me in surprised silence.

"I don't think you understand what I said," Dr. McCormick stated.

"No, I don't think you understand what I said." In spite of his dire announcement, God's voice still resonated in my spirit.

With the support of my family, I decided to stay at Saint Vincent's for the surgery. It was scheduled for the end of the week.

As I waited for my procedure, God's plan become ever clearer to me. I knew I was being prepared as he showed me his new mission for my life.

I knew with certainty he wanted to use my situation to deliver a message that would bring people closer to him—a message of hope, faith, encouragement, and inner change.

"I can't believe his attitude," said everyone who stopped by to visit me. They didn't understand it wasn't really me. God was carrying me and preparing me for a new life. I was simply a reflection of his love, his purpose, and most of all, his grace.

It was one thing to hear God's voice when I was sedated and another when his plan started to unfold. His message was not a dream.

The voice of the Lord is powerful; the voice of the Lord is majestic. PSALM 29:4

8

Surrounded by Love

Love is always bestowed as a gift—freely,
willingly and without expectation.
We don't love to be loved; we love to love.

LEO BUSCAGLIA

After a few days of being alert enough to speak and make sense, I asked Anita to contact my residents and tell them I planned to continue overseeing their medical education.

"I already did," she said, understanding the importance of making my wishes known. "You wrote a note when you were on the respirator."

I didn't remember doing that.

Later that day, they all came to visit me as a group. Each took a spot around my hospital bed until there was no place left to stand.

Seeing their sullen faces, I wanted to cry, but I held in my emotions. I felt it was crucial to not break the bond of trust between us. I didn't want to cave in and create any fear of abandonment for them.

"I know I'm paralyzed," I said in a matter-of-fact tone. "And I know you know I'm paralyzed. But I haven't forgotten my responsibility to educate you as OB/GYN residents. I will make sure your education is not compromised. All of you will complete your graduation requirements. I promise this. You can count on it."

As I talked, my breathing became labored. An X-ray taken earlier that morning had revealed blood in my left lung. I needed a chest tube inserted. When the hospital's surgical resident arrived to do the procedure, he asked everyone to leave.

"No, they need to stay and see this," I insisted. "Their observations can be noted in their year-end log as a witnessed procedure." Observing surgeries is a requirement before residents can perform them under supervision.

The surgeon hesitantly gave his approval, and my residents stayed. A few almost fainted when they saw blood spurting against the walls of the room. But it was a great learning experience.

Anita had purchased a memory book for visitors to sign. Every resident wrote something in the book before leaving. They filled the pages with expressions of encouragement, love, and appreciation.

Dr. Bernado, my lung specialist, came into my room after the procedure. "You've really touched the lives of your residents. I've never seen anything like it."

"I'm the lucky one," I said. "I've never seen a physician touched as deeply by his residents as I have been."

I'd always realized that the work I'm called to do is important. But being in a life-threatening situation gave me the privilege of hearing, seeing, and feeling the kind of love people usually express for someone after they're gone forever—at their funeral or memorial, through testimonies and eulogies. I was alive to receive these precious gifts of love from people whose lives I'd touched.

More than 1,700 cards and letters poured in during my two-week hospital stay. Flowers, gifts, and phone calls arrived daily. The outpouring of love was unbelievable.

One afternoon, Dr. Ray Deiter, a former resident of mine, called. "How's your insurance?"

"Okay, I guess. Why do you ask?"

"Do you have good disability coverage?"

"I'm pretty sure I do." In truth, I hadn't even thought of that.

"Well, if you don't have enough, I'm prepared to give you a hundred thousand dollars to help pay for your expenses."

Tears came to my eyes. "Are you kidding me?"

"I can't give you your legs back, David. But I can at least give you some money to help pay for your rehab."

I couldn't believe anyone would do this. I didn't accept the money, as my insurance covered what I needed. But I will never forget his sincere intention and generosity.

Another former resident, my friend and colleague Dr. Paul Krueger, flew in from New Jersey to visit me. I was surprised that he'd been able to take time away from his busy practice to come see me. Standing beside my bed, he stared at the ring on his finger. It had been presented to him in March 2001, when he was elected president of the American College of Osteopathic Obstetricians and Gynecologists. It represented his pride in the college and his position.

With solemn assurance, he removed the ring from his finger. "David, I want you to wear this." He spoke with a confident voice. "Please accept it as a symbol of your future return to the college. And to remind you to focus on becoming one of our next presidents. You're the kind of person we need for the job."

I told him I couldn't take the ring. It wasn't the right thing to do. But his gesture had a profound effect on my determination to press on.

Before leaving, he reminded me of my difficult climb back to the top of the mountain. "Remember: two steps forward, one step back, but always stay focused on the forward step." He gave me a supportive hug. "I'll be seeing you soon, David."

God clearly spoke his love through this kind, loving, loyal friend. Paul was a gift of hope and encouragement that humbled me with gratitude and a reminder to never give up.

> **If anyone gives even a cup of cold water to one of these little ones because he is my disciple, I tell you the truth, he will certainly not lose his reward.** MATTHEW 10:42

Several of my prior patients came by to visit me. They reminisced about times when I'd made a difference in their lives. Because of the thousands of patients I'd seen since beginning my medical practice, I couldn't remember many of those times. But it meant a great deal to me that they remembered me.

One patient shared how I stayed with her all night at the hospital when her baby died. Another reminded me of a time when I spent two hours with her in the exam room. She needed someone to talk to during a rough period in her life. I spent a great deal of time listening to her, even though there was a waiting room full of patients who needed to be seen.

I often prayed with my patients and encouraged them to use the chapel in my medical office for their prayer needs. This had always seemed normal to me. According to my patients, my approach wasn't typical.

One evening, my family went out for a dinner break. I was alone in my hospital room. Being on a morphine drip caused me to drift off, but I wasn't really asleep. I could hear the nurses chattering and the clanking of food-service carts being wheeled from room to room.

At one point, I opened my eyes and saw a woman in a beautiful pink sweater standing by my bedside, gently rubbing my shoulder. Silent tears streamed down her cheeks. I recognized her as Sheri, one of my patients.

"Why are you crying?" I asked quietly.

"Because you're so sick."

My heart grieved for her, as I knew she had advanced breast cancer.

"Sheri, we should pray for you. Would that be okay?"

"Dr. Wolf, you always direct the conversation away from yourself and back to me." Her eyes were full of sadness and love.

After we prayed together, she showed me a terrarium filled with beautiful living plants that she'd brought as a gift. But her real gifts were compassion and friendship.

Being alone in my hospital room at night was frightening. Horrible thoughts clouded my mind.

What if I stop breathing and the respirator alarm doesn't go off?

What if I can't reach my call button, so the nurses don't come in here?

What if I die?

One night I decided to hold my breath long enough to make the alarm go off. It seemed like an eternity before help arrived. A nurse showed up and assessed the situation quickly.

"Dr. Wolf, the equipment is working just fine and we're monitoring you closely," she said gently. "There's no need to test us."

Scared to death, I turned to prayer.

Thank you, God, for your grace. And for the tremendous patience in the hearts of the nursing staff. They understand, even when I'm not alert enough to know what I'm doing—which is most of the time.

Mornings were a relief because I knew my family would return. I was always eager for Anita and Sue to show up. They were the most important people during my time in ICU, witnessing each day as I struggled to regain my identity.

Anita provided a kind of tough love by not automatically doing everything I asked her to do. She wanted me to become independent again, knowing it meant a better life down the road for both of us.

To be honest, I didn't like that at first. I kept thinking, *Gee, Anita, can't you at least get me a pencil or a Kleenex? This isn't easy for me, you know!*

Of course, she knew. Anita knew better than anyone and didn't want me to get in the habit of feeling helpless. It was her way of motivating me—and keeping up my confidence. She was prepared to be in this thing forever, and she didn't want either one of us to become victims of our circumstances.

Sue showed her love very differently. She wanted to provide care by doing little things that mattered to me. Every day she read me the Bible, washed my hair, opened stacks of mail, and read every card and letter out loud. These things became part of our daily routine.

When my emotions got the better of me, she let me cry on her shoulder. She did anything I asked her to do. I liked that a lot!

After the first week, everyone in my family had to leave. Anita went back to work at Riverside Osteopathic Hospital, to fulfill her duties as an RN. Raquel returned to graduate school at the University of Saint Louis.

And Brad resumed his studies at Western Michigan University.

It was hard to let them go, but it was even more difficult letting Sue go. She'd provided comfort in many ways. Her love was gentle and soothing.

And I was more dependent on her than I realized until she was gone.

My only salvation was remembering a passage from *My Utmost for His Highest* by Oswald Chambers, a devotional book given to me several years earlier:

My sister, Sue Green, and her husband, Larry

> It is not wrong for you to depend on your Elijah for as long as God gives him to you, but remember that the time will come when he must leave and no longer be your guide and your leader, for God does not intend for him to stay. Even the thought of death will cause you to say, "I can't continue without my Elijah," but God says you must continue.[2]

Elijah was God's servant. He gave Elijah power to create miracles that provided hope and encouragement for struggling people.

Sue was my Elijah.

I took consolation in a paper Anita had tacked on the wall next to my bed to keep my confidence up. It was a writing assignment Brad had been given in college, before my accident, to describe his role model. It was titled "My Father," and he wrote purely from his heart.

My father stands ten feet tall to me. In reality he is only 5 foot 7 inches, but his heart is twice the size of his body. He is stocky and fair skinned, with dark graying hair. His smile lights up the room and you can see his soul when you look into his eyes. He wears a mask of confidence, but he doesn't let that get in the way of people seeing his real face. The best quality about him is that he wears his heart on his sleeve.

All of these things don't even shed a light on my father's good qualities. His job is to help people, and in a way to create miracles. You see, my father is a doctor. He delivers babies. He treats his patients as if he has known them all of his life. He doesn't just give them medical help; he does his best to help them with all of their problems.

As you can see, I think the world of my father. Other people do too.

(See Appendix 1 for entire text.)

Brad's paper was a constant reminder of his love for and pride in me. I gazed at it several times a day during my two-week hospital stay. Each time boosted my sagging confidence, if only for a little while.

I've always been a confident man. Having to rely on others as a patient didn't set well with my take-charge personality. I wanted to be in control.

9

Grace

*Anything under God's control
is never out of control.*

CHARLES SWINDOLL

My case was especially challenging for the care team at Saint Vincent's because I'm a doctor. I've been taught the science of medicine. I'm a critical thinker, and I'm used to giving orders. Making persistent demands seemed natural to me.

My family was alerted once my two o'clock surgery time was set. But the transporter showed up in my room earlier than expected.

"Anita hasn't arrived yet, and there's no way I'm going to surgery without her here."

The hospital staff accommodated me. The surgery was delayed until Anita showed up.

During the wait, I questioned the anesthesiologist and nurses about their credentials and experience. Checking them out gave me reassurance and a sense of control.

God probably smiled about that. I had a lot to learn about control.

> **He looks down on all who are haughty; he is king over all that are proud.** JOB 41:34

The surgery went well. Several days later, I was measured for a "turtle brace" to stabilize my back. These hard plastic braces come in two pieces and are fitted from armpits to groin and secured with large, tightly wrapped Velcro straps.

The surgeon told me I'd have to wear that miserable thing anytime I wanted to sit up. To get it on, someone had to roll me onto my side to put on the back piece first, then roll me onto my back to attach the front piece. It could only be removed when I was lying down. What a cumbersome nuisance.

I hated feeling confined, but my better judgment followed the doctor's orders.

To make matters worse, the radiology report stated my neck was broken. I was sure the report was wrong. But my doctor insisted I wear a neck collar. It pushed against my chin, making it difficult to move my head up and down. It drove me nuts!

It was bad enough having a chest tube, catheters, multiple IV lines, and a turtle brace, but the collar was the last straw. I had to prove I was right about the X-rays.

When the resident showed up around five the next morning, I insisted my neck wasn't broken.

"I don't know, Dr. Wolf," he said. "Your X-rays indicated—"

"I need more X-rays. Can you help?"

He hesitated, then nodded. "I guess we can bend the rules this time."

The best position for me to get the pictures I needed was sitting with my shoulders pushed down. Knowing the pain would be unbearable, I used my morphine pump to give myself some relief.

It took more than one set of films to get perfect pictures, but we did it. And the results proved that my neck wasn't broken!

Unfortunately, Dr. McCormick wasn't there to approve the collar removal. So once again, I convinced the resident to go the extra mile. He called Dr. McCormick, who gave approval over the phone.

What a relief to finally have the collar off!

I shook the resident's hand before he continued his morning rounds. "I appreciate your extra effort to help me. You're a lifesaver!"

"No problem, Dr. Wolf. I'm glad this worked out for you."

After he left, I prayed.

Thank you, God, for your grace today. Your heart and hands are working through many people.

I was forbidden to get out of bed, but I knew if I didn't get up, I would start losing body function. I always wrote orders for my hospital patients to get up right away, knowing it's the best thing for a speedy recovery.

When I argued, my nurse said, "But you'll get dizzy if you get up. You may even faint."

Again, I disagreed.

Against doctor's orders, I convinced the nurse to lift me out of bed and sit me on a chair. I got a little dizzy, but I didn't faint.

Supported by the turtle brace, I sat up as straight as possible when Dr. McCormick came in to see me next.

He couldn't believe his eyes. "You're one amazing man, Dr. Wolf."

At least my determination and persuasive talents were still alive and well.

On my seventh day in the hospital, I started getting concerned about the removal of my chest tube. It had to be taken out before I could be released to rehab.

My son-in-law, Marc, who was working on his master's degree in physical therapy, took charge of evaluating my rehab options. After investigating locations over the Internet, he found two places near my home: the University of Michigan Physical Medicine and Rehabilitation Clinic in Ann Arbor and the Rehabilitation Institute of Michigan at the Wayne State University School of Medicine in Detroit. Marc and Raquel visited both sites, then chose RIM for three reasons:

1. Dr. Edward Nieshoff, RIM's spinal-cord-injury specialist, is also paralyzed. He is known for his advocacy in fighting for the rights of people with disabilities.

2. RIM had large private rooms, with home-style décor, unlike standard hospital-room furnishings, so I'd have a nice setting to spend time with visitors.

3. I wanted to see Anita every day. RIM's closer location made this easier.

As a family, we agreed that RIM provided the best solution to meet our needs. Raquel reserved a room for me.

Determined to expedite matters, I called my trusted friend Dr. Laskowski, a thoracic surgeon, and asked for his advice.

"Negotiate with your trauma surgeon to have your chest tube removed by the fourteenth day," he advised. "If that doesn't work, I'd recommend that you get a thoracic surgery consult."

When Dr. Navakovic, my trauma surgeon, arrived, I asked, "What's the plan for removing my chest tube?"

"There's no rush, Dr. Wolf," she stated in her calm physician manner. "I'll let you know when it's time to remove it."

"I want to go to rehab in a week. RIM is expecting me, and I don't want to lose the room I've reserved."

"I didn't know you already made plans for rehab," she said in surprise.

"If my chest tube isn't taken out by the fourteenth day, I'd like to get a thoracic surgeon consult. Will you agree to this?"

"I'll allow it."

The chest tube was removed on the thirteenth day, with no problems. The next thing on my agenda: discharge.

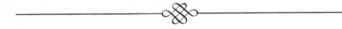

In spite of my determined personality, God's hands were in everything I experienced during my hospital stay. As I embraced the outpouring of love, compassion, and excellent care from family, friends, and clinical staff, my heart was being humbled. I had to learn that God is truly the only one in control. And all good things come in his timing.

Humble yourselves, therefore, under God's mighty hand, that he may lift you up in due time. 1 PETER 5:6

10

God's Timing

Once in a while you get shown the light in
the strangest of places, if you look at it right.
JERRY GARCIA

During my two-week hospital stay, which felt like it lasted two years, I had a lot of time with nothing to do but think. I found myself pondering the journey God had taken me on that led to this point in my life.

I've wanted to be a doctor for as long as I can remember. The first vision of this calling came to me in the fourth grade. As a sophomore at Kokomo High School in Indiana, I decided to become an OB/GYN physician. My parents were all for it.

Mom realized that more than my dad's income was needed to help make my dream come true. With a positive attitude, she enrolled in beauty school. After getting her hairdresser's license, she opened a shop in our home. This gave her an opportunity to make extra money for my college education and still be there to keep an eye on my sister and me.

Mom and Dad prayed often. They believed that with God, hard work, and discipline, a person could do almost anything. They were right!

During my junior year in high school, Dad's brother, Uncle Claude, asked me where I planned to attend college.

"I want to go to Indiana University in Bloomington," I said with pride. "It's the biggest school in the state."

"Bigger doesn't necessarily mean better." Uncle Claude was head basketball coach at a much smaller college in Indiana and wanted me to check out his school. "How about coming to Manchester for a weekend and letting me show you around?" Besides being a coach, he was an ordained minister in the Church of the Brethren. I was sure this meant I wouldn't miss Sunday service.

Even though my mind was pretty much made up, I said yes. I loved and respected him and trusted his wise counsel. Next to my mom and dad, Uncle Claude and his wife, Aunt June, were my closest mentors.

My parents drove me forty miles to their home for a visit on a Saturday afternoon. While they chatted with Aunt June, Uncle Claude gave me a VIP tour of the college. He told me about the great science department, the exceptional pre-med program, and the strong Christian presence on campus. Everything he said appealed to me.

He emphasized the importance of having a religious influence during my maturing years. "I believe this small Christian college suits you, David," he said with confidence.

I started rethinking my plan.

After the tour we met with Dr. Weimer, chairman of the chemistry department. He spent an hour talking with me. He was clearly a man dedicated to his work. My future seemed important to him. I left his office with a different attitude about the school but still wasn't sure it was the right fit for me.

After the two of us returned to Uncle Claude's home, we all ate supper together and discussed my thoughts about the college and how they matched up with my goals. The tour and my good impression of Dr. Weimer made a difference, but they were not the most important considerations.

Although well known and respected, Indiana University didn't have the strong underpinning of faith and family available to me at Manchester College. My decision to attend the college was made by values instilled in me through deep family roots.

In addition, though Manchester didn't have the star power of Indiana University, it had something money can't buy: two people who would be there for me, ready, willing, and able to guide and encourage me through the demands of collegiate academic life and the beginning of my new independence away from home.

I was accepted into Manchester's pre-med program. During the spring of my junior year, I took the Medical College Admissions Test (MCAT) in preparation for medical school. I was certain I aced the test, but when my scores were posted, I discovered they were average. Needless to say, I was disappointed.

My poor scores resulted in rejection from medical school. I was devastated. *What am I going to do with a double major in biology and chemistry? I've wasted three years.*

I started questioning God. *You know I want to be a doctor. I thought that's what you wanted too. Why did you tell me to do this when I was nine? Why have you let me go this far only to slam the door in my face?*

I walked the campus at night, looking up into the starry sky, asking God hard questions. Are you there? Do I matter to you? Is there a reason you're doing this?

There was only one person I could turn to: Uncle Claude.

When I called, he was taking care of Aunt June on her first day home after hysterectomy surgery. She was his top priority, but he could hear the frustration in my voice when I whimpered, "My acceptance into medical school was declined."

"Everything is going to work out," he reassured me. "Why don't you come over so we can talk about this?"

Grateful for his willingness to meet with me, I hurried over.

"I've wanted to be a doctor since I was in fourth grade," I said, pouring out my heart. "Nothing else interests me."

"I think you should pursue a career in social work."

"I don't know anything about social work. My pre-med courses have been focused on science, not people. I've only had one psychology class and no classes in sociology." I sighed. "Maybe I can be a minister," I said, grasping at straws.

"I think you're better suited for social work. I can ask Dr. Evans, chairman of the sociology department, to talk with you. Will you allow me to call him?"

How could I say no to my uncle? "Okay." But I doubted Dr. Evans could help.

As I started to leave, he said, "Let's pray."

We bowed our heads.

"Dear Lord, thank you for your presence today. This is a troubled time for David—a time of doubt and turmoil. Please help him learn to trust you and have faith in your plan for his life. Guide him with your wisdom so he will receive a positive result from the decision he makes about his future education. Guard him against any negative emotions and keep him strong when he is tempted to give up. In Jesus' name I pray. Amen."

They cried to you and were saved; in you they trusted and were not disappointed. PSALM 22:5

Our conversation and his prayer meant a great deal to me. Though I was still confused, it helped to have an option as well as the peace that comes with prayer.

I needed someone who cared enough to help me see new possibilities. The worst thing in the world is to be alone with a problem. God knows who to send when we seem to hit a dead end.

Dr. Evans and I met the next day.

"Coach Wolf told me about your disappointment." His tone carried empathy.

"I'm confused," I blurted out. "I've never wanted to be anything but a doctor."

"I understand. But you're open to the possibility of social work?"

"I don't know anything about it, but I'm willing to give it a try. What school do you recommend?"

"Indiana University has a great master's program and excellent professors." How ironic that he would recommend my first-choice college. "I'll be happy to write you a letter of recommendation."

"Thank you," I said in surprise. He didn't even know me. His offer was given due to the relationship between him and my Uncle Claude.

Dad took me to the university to meet with Dr. Lawrence, the dean of social work. My application was accepted. Relieved that my life wasn't over after all, I was able to concentrate on my continued studies at Manchester College.

I graduated in June 1969 with mixed feelings: proud of my diploma, but sad to be leaving Uncle Claude and Aunt June. It was an emotional good-bye.

Ever since high school, my summer vacations had been spent working to earn extra spending money for the next school year. But the summer between my first and second year of graduate school was different. I had to prepare for my second MCAT.

When I picked up my year-end paper at the social-work office, my professor, Dr. Taylor, was there, wrapping up semester details. With a genuine smile, she handed me my paper. "See you next fall, *Dr. Wolf.*"

Apparently she assumed I was planning to pursue a Doctor of Social Work degree. "Oh, I think an MSW will be enough for me."

She smiled. "I understand. But I know you want to be a doctor. And you should always follow your dream."

Goose bumps raced up and down my spine. I had never discussed with her my goal of becoming a doctor. Had God prompted her to say this? Her comment was exactly the encouragement I needed. "Thanks, Dr. Taylor." My voice quivered. "I'm going to study hard for the MCAT. I'm going to make it this time!"

I went to the library every day that summer and studied like crazy.

When fall arrived, I continued my second year in the master's program. That spring I earned my MSW from Indiana University and passed the MCAT—with flying colors.

Once again, I applied to medical school, and this time I was accepted at Des Moines University College of Osteopathic Medicine in Iowa. I completed my internship and OB/GYN residency at Riverside Osteopathic Hospital in Trenton, Michigan.

In 1979, I went into practice with Dr. Harvey Orth, a memorable mentor. In 1984, I started my own medical clinic with the help of Laurie Meadows.

My business grew rapidly through word-of-mouth referrals. We soon needed a bigger building to handle the growing number of patients and staff. I purchased property one block from the hospital and started drawing up plans for the building.

A man showed up unannounced in my office one day. My receptionist told him I was busy seeing patients and suggested he make an appointment. But he refused to leave.

Between patients, my receptionist told me about the persistent man in the waiting room. Curious, I went out to see him. "I'm Dr. Wolf." Noticing his attire, I asked, "Are you bidding on the new building?"

He stood. "I'm Frank Haikus. I'm a contractor, and I'd like to take you to lunch."

"I don't need you to buy my lunch to discuss the project."

"Hey, I don't need the job. I just want to share a meal with you and find out what kind of a building you're thinking about."

I agreed to go with him. He paid for his food. I paid for mine.

Frank and I had more than one conversation before I figured he was right for the job. I liked his honest, straightforward, no-nonsense, down-to-earth approach to life and work. His years of general-contractor experience impressed me, and he had glowing recommendations from past clients. I felt comfortable with him. On a handshake, we agreed to be partners for the project.

But frustration mounted shortly after construction began. The city required soil sampling, and the results showed the soil was contaminated with petroleum products. Not too surprising since a gas station previously occupied the property. We were concerned about a potential health problem and hired an independent company, suggested by the Environmental Protection Agency, to conduct further testing.

To make matters worse, bricklayers placed the wrong bricks on the building—twice. And a bulldozer severed a major gas line, threatening a whole city block. Construction came to a standstill for eight weeks.

I prayed about the situation, the way Mom and Dad had taught me. But I needed more than a few quick prayers to discern God's direction.

About that time, Anita and I received an invitation from Dr. James Dobson's Focus on the Family to attend a four-day conference for Christian physicians, to be held in Colorado Springs. We decided to attend.

I was impressed that each building on Dr. Dobson's campus was dedicated to God. Plaques on the front of the buildings said, "May God always be glorified in this place." The building where the conference was held had a beautiful chapel—a place of solitude and prayer for employees, friends, and guests.

My mind drifted to the problems we were having with the construction project. "Maybe I'm not supposed to have my own medical facility," I told Anita. "God probably wants our money spent somewhere else."

"I don't think so, Dave. I believe God wants you to dedicate your building to him, the same way Dr. Dobson has."

Anita's words simmered in my heart and mind during the flight back to Detroit. I thanked the Lord for this awesome experience and for my wonderful wife and her insight.

God's voice interrupted my prayer. *David, you have been growing your practice and trying to construct this building for the wrong reasons. You have great skills, but I am the one who has given them to you. You are taking care of my patients, not yours. And now I want you to recognize that your building belongs to me as well.*

Between God and Anita, I got the message loud and clear!

Shortly after arriving home, construction obstacles began to disappear. And I gave all the glory to God.

I started planning an inspirational building-dedication ceremony. I couldn't wait to announce my new focus to the community and especially to my staff. I wanted it to be a pep rally for God!

More than fifty people attended the dedication, held in the large waiting area of the new office. My eyes filled with tears as I began my message.

"As you all know, medicine is an important part of my life. But God is even more important to me. So this is not a 'welcome to the building' ceremony. Nor is it an open house. This is an official dedication of this building to Jesus Christ."

Guests smiled and applauded. Some had tears in their eyes.

"Construction has not been easy. But God had his eye on this project since we broke ground with the first shovel of dirt. Thanks to his timing, I've learned two things. First, this building is his, not mine. And second, the patients who come here are also his."

I pointed to Anita as I continued.

"We would not be here today if God had not placed words in Anita's mouth for me to hear. The plaque mounted on the brick wall outside the building entrance, where people can see it as they enter, was her idea and God's intention for the building. God and Anita have always been the guiding lights in my life."

My wife and I exchanged a loving glance.

"I am proud to follow Dr. James Dobson's humble example with this beautiful bronze dedication plaque that says, 'To GOD and the caring of women and their unborn babies.'"

I turned to my employees, who were standing in a group by the opening to the exam-room area. "I am committed to the words on this plaque. I'm confident that you are too. I hope, every day when you come to work, you are aware of your higher purpose. God will be glorified here. Thank you, and God bless you."

Soon after the building opened, I announced plans for adding a chapel in the basement. It would be available for prayer and meditation anytime the building was open.

I insisted on real pews. But Frank, my trusted friend and advisor, informed me that he had no experience building church pews.

"Most churches require several large pews. Since the chapel is small, we only need two short ones—fifty-one and a half inches, to be exact. This could cost a bundle, because they will probably have to be custom made."

Frank knew this was important to me. So he put out feelers all over town to get what we needed.

Two weeks later he said, "I'm having trouble finding the resources to get the job done."

"I can't believe no one wants to build those pews. Someone's got to be willing to help."

One night, Father Jim Vedro from Saint Joseph Catholic Church stopped by my office to see me. "I heard through the grapevine you're looking for some pews for your new chapel."

I confirmed the rumor.

"Our church convent is being dismantled, and we'd like to offer you the convent chapel pews, if you still need some."

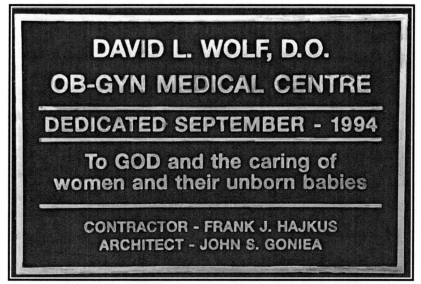

The God-inspired dedication plaque placed at the entrance of my medical building

I doubted his pews would be the right size, but accepted his invitation to look them over.

The following day, tape measure in hand, Frank and I went to measure the pews. There were just two—and they were exactly the size we needed.

I immediately called Father Vedro. "How much do you want for them?"

"That's between you and God."

His response caught me off guard. How could I put a price on something this valuable to me? I didn't know what was fair.

Before I could suggest a price, Father Vedro also offered me two wall statues, hand-carved in Italy, and a large cross for above the chapel altar. Again he insisted the decision on price was between me and God. This added to my dilemma over how much to pay. I prayed for several days before figuring out that one. I decided to give him two thousand dollars. He was pleased.

After the exchange, Frank installed the pews, mounted the statues, and hung the cross. Seeing the results reinforced my knowledge of God's will and timing for the building.

Over the years, patients, staff, and many others have used the chapel as a place of solitude for their spiritual needs. It became a place of refuge and a recognized symbol of God's love and the power of his unfailing grace. It served as a vital part of my medical practice.

This beautiful medical building became a house of God due to my willingness to follow the vision he provided. Tangible reflections of him are in every room, and a Bible is kept in the waiting room. His presence is felt during intimate conversations with patients behind closed exam-room doors. Most of these talks center on Jesus and his power to help with life's challenges.

His timing for the events in my life continues to amaze me!

11

Wake-Up Call

Fear will always knock at your door.
Just don't invite it in for dinner.
MAX LUCADO

Finally my two-week hospital stay ended. An attendant helped Anita dress me and wrap my turtle brace securely around my torso. They wheeled my gurney to the hospital entrance, where two ambulance attendants transferred me to a portable bed.

I wanted to express my thanks to the many special people who'd gone above and beyond, contending with my forceful persuasiveness and demands. Day and night, they gave me the best care possible. These people had kept me functioning!

Streams of uncontrollable tears flowed with every hug and handshake. Words were few, but my appreciation was undeniable. My weakened physical condition heightened my emotions, along with the knowledge that I had a long journey ahead.

As I rode in the back of the ambulance to the Rehabilitation Institute of Michigan, I felt scared and alone. I didn't like being separated from my wife. I could see her driving the SUV behind us, but I ached to hold her hand.

All of a sudden, I was hit hard by a thought. *I can no longer rely on anyone else to help with the next part of my recovery.* At rehab I would have no sister washing my hair or reading the Bible to me. No Anita, no Brad, no Raquel. They would come to visit, but their work and school schedules were important. I'd have no familiar hospital staff to indulge me or fall for my persuasion tactics. Now it was all up to me and the grace of God. An enormous rush of emotions poured over me.

During the hour-long ambulance ride, I started to recognize the possibility that many of my hopes and dreams had just been shattered.

My mind flashed back to my marriage proposal to Anita. It was a beautiful day in October 1970. I was in my last year of graduate school. She was a registered nurse. Our five-year courtship was long enough for me to know she was "the right one." I wanted my proposal to be a surprise, so I nonchalantly asked her to go for a Saturday walk in the park. We took walks in the park often, so my question was nothing out of the ordinary.

We held hands and shuffled through the falling leaves. Our eyes feasted on the glorious autumn colors and sparkled with young love. We laughed and talked about our dreams. Life was full of hope and promise for a bright future.

In a burst of joy, I dropped to one knee, clasping my hands around Anita's. She looked a little startled as I began my speech.

"Today is a special day—one I have been imagining for some time now. I admire your determination and Christian character. And I love your caring personality. You are a wonderful person, and I'm blessed to know you. I want you to be my wife." Before she could respond, I added, "But there are some things you must understand. God is first in my life. When I become a doctor, my patients will be second. You will be third. But I love you. I love you very much. Will you marry me?"

Anita beamed with joy and confidence. "David, I know who you are and what you are made of. Yes, I will marry you!"

I was thrilled.

We were married on July 17, 1971, two months before I started medical school. Uncle Claude conducted the ceremony at the Church of the Brethren in Kokomo. It was the launch of a wonderful lifelong adventure.

But lying in the ambulance I realized that adventure was now covered by a great disappointment for me—and for Anita.

From the beginning of our marriage, my wife always followed my greatest desires.

Anita patiently waited seven days for our Hawaiian honeymoon cruise to get under way. I spent the first week of our marriage on a fishing trip with my dad, his brother (my Uncle Earl), and my Grandfather Wolf, while Anita stayed with my mother. She never once complained.

We lived in a small apartment during medical school. I used one of the two tiny bedrooms as an office. I made a DO NOT DISTURB sign and hung it on the doorknob when I was studying—which was most of the time. Anita was alone many hours. It was a taste of what life would be like as Mrs. Wolf. Again, she never complained.

Anita even took on extra nursing shifts to help pay for my medical education—and still did not complain.

When I went into practice, she handled the household responsibilities. And when the kids were born, she managed all family matters. As always, she never complained.

God created few women like Anita. Above all, she loves God. And her family is a top priority.

Confined in the ambulance, I wondered how Anita would handle this new life that had suddenly been thrust upon us. I knew her well enough to realize that she would persevere without complaint. Yet tears filled my eyes. I waved pathetically out the back windows of the ambulance. With a tender smile, she waved back.

Questions continued whirling in my head. *Can I accept a wheelchair as my new means of mobility? Can I learn to transfer by myself? Will I have the strength to do it? How will I handle being a patient this time?*

Fear of the unknown magnified my concerns. Though I had much love and support from family and friends, I was now solely responsible for determining whether I would fail or succeed. It was a jarring wake-up call.

I knew I had to trust in God's timing. His power and grace would be crucial for the next steps in my journey with Jesus.

I was so caught up in my own emotions, I couldn't even pray. Prayer is what I needed most, but fear gave Satan the advantage.

For I am the Lord, your God, who takes hold of your right hand and says to you, Do not fear; I will help you.
Isaiah 41:13

When we arrived at RIM, the ambulance attendants waited for Anita to park before wheeling me on the gurney through the main entrance. I was anxious and wondered whether everyone there would be in wheelchairs.

I felt a little better once Anita got there. She held my hand as a couple of expressionless employees directed us to the elevators. None of the busy hospital workers even gave me a passing glance.

My anxiety mounted during the silent elevator ride to the fourth-floor spinal-cord-injury unit. When the metal door opened, my fears were confirmed. Everyone I saw was in a wheelchair. I didn't want to be identified that way.

While most of the patients were dressed in T-shirts and sweats, one man wore a shirt and tie. He was talking to another staff person. As soon as he noticed me, he wheeled over to me with a big smile. "Hello, David. I'm Dr. Nieshoff. Everyone around here calls me Ed."

I won't be calling you Ed. And you won't be calling me David! I thought my identity would be preserved if he called me Dr. Wolf.

He led me to my new room. As Raquel had promised, it was spacious and private and not decorated like a typical hospital room. It looked more like a hotel suite with floor-to-ceiling draperies, dark hardwood-type floors, and a small conference table with four fabric-covered chairs. The green and blue colors were soothing. I expected to see the television, but was surprised to see a microwave oven and refrigerator. My favorite area was the bathroom, with a large roll-in shower. Everything looked and smelled fresh, like a maid service had prepared for my arrival. I was comfortable with my new surroundings and felt that visitors would be comfortable too.

After the ambulance tech and a nurse assistant transferred me from the gurney to the bed, my body sank into the mattress. Anita elevated the head of the electric bed and positioned my pillow to make me as comfortable as possible. Then she pulled up a chair and sat next to me as we mindlessly watched TV. The day had already been long and exhausting, but it wasn't over yet.

An hour later the rehab team came to my room and introduced themselves. Dr. Nieshoff led the core team, which included a physical therapist, an occupational therapist, a recreational therapist, and a nurse.

All smiles with my rehab team at the Rehabilitation Institute of Michigan after I was honored with the Distinguished Alumnus Award, September 27, 2010 (Left to right: Janine, physical therapist; Dr. Edward Nieshoff, director; Diane, occupational therapist; me; and Gabbie, physical therapist)

Their professionalism and friendliness surprised me after what I had felt on my way up to the unit. I appreciated their courtesy and respect. It's the way I've always treated my patients to make them feel important and not like a number.

As the group turned to leave, Dr. Nieshoff assured me, "We'll be back in two hours for a family conference to discuss your rehab goals and treatment plan."

"Okay," I said eagerly. I was ready to hear their goals and share some of my own!

The team returned as scheduled to discuss my treatment plan. Dr. Nieshoff sat at the conference table with Anita and explained the details to me while I remained in bed.

"David, you will be receiving physical therapy and occupational therapy every day. Our first goal is to teach you how to transfer to and from a wheelchair. Then we will make sure you can accomplish the standard activities of daily living, such as showering on your own, putting your clothes on and taking them off by yourself, and so on. The plan can be modified if it becomes too aggressive for you."

Are you kidding me? There's no way your plan will be too aggressive for me!

Before finalizing the plan, Dr. Nieshoff asked about my personal rehab goals.

I'm sure the team expected me to say, *"I want to get out of this bed into a wheelchair."* Instead, I said, "I have two goals. One, I want to continue being an OB/GYN physician. Two, I want to go to the Norte Dame–Purdue football game this fall." They kept their feelings hidden behind poker faces, but I suspected they thought I was being overly optimistic.

"When is the game?" Dr. Nieshoff asked.

"September fifteenth." That was less than a month away!

Eyes widened, eyebrows raised, and jaws dropped as the team tried to maintain their composure.

"It won't be because of me if I don't make it. I want you to push me hard. I want the maximum amount of rehab right from day one."

"I can't make any promises," Dr. Nieshoff said empathetically. "But we'll do our best to make this happen. You are the exception to the rule around here."

Diane, the occupational therapist, smiled and validated Dr. Nieshoff's comment. "We're not used to having patients with aggressive goals," she said with enthusiasm. "You should be proud of yourself."

"Thanks. I'm serious about this."

"Good! That's what I like to hear." She gave me a thumbs-up. "What time do you usually get up in the morning?"

"About six o'clock on a normal day."

"Perfect. I'll see you tomorrow at six."

"Are you kidding?" No one had gotten me up that early at Saint Vincent's.

"No."

"What are we going to do that early in the morning?"

"I'll be getting you up and into the shower. And you're going to shave at the sink in front of the mirror."

"I haven't been in the shower since my accident. The nurses at the hospital bathed me and washed my hair in bed."

"I know." She smiled. "But that's not going to happen anymore."

I couldn't argue with her. This is exactly what I said I wanted.

I looked into the faces of the team members surrounding my bed. "I have one final request. Could you please call me Dr. Wolf?" My shaken confidence needed an identity boost.

"Of course," they all responded. "Absolutely no problem."

When evening came, Anita had to leave. I was scared and didn't want her to go. But we both knew that without her there, I had a better chance of staying focused the next day.

Moments after our tear-filled departure, I fell asleep from sheer exhaustion.

12

Embracing My New Reality

The greatest power we need in our lives is to begin again.
KERRY SHOOK

I woke up feeling like I was watching a movie in slow motion. A wheelchair sat beside my bed, and I wondered why it was there. *Who does that belong to?*

Suddenly it hit me. *It's mine!*

I stared at it. *I don't need that. I'm going to walk again.*

I'd always been a competitor. Competitors believe that with hard work and determination, anything is possible.

But the wheelchair and I had a reckoning that morning. We decided to be friends—at least for a while.

Physical therapy started at ten o'clock. I had to roll myself to the elevators and get to the gym on the floor below, which was no small feat—especially since I was required to wear my turtle brace during all components of rehab, as it was the only way to ensure my back was stabilized.

Janine, my PT, was waiting with a smile when I arrived. "Today we're going to practice getting in and out of the wheelchair," she said in a positive tone.

You've got to be kidding me! Just transferring myself from the bed to my wheelchair was exhausting.

"I want you to roll up parallel to the table. Remove the wheelchair arm and footplate closest to the table, and slide your bottom over as close as you can get to it. Then lift yourself onto the table."

The table was the height of my wheelchair seat and covered with a gym mat. Her instructions seemed simple. But doing the exercise was tougher than I expected. I quickly became frustrated and extremely tired. "Can I take a break?" I pleaded.

"No. You asked us to push you hard. And that's what I'm doing."

I knew she was right. I had to stay focused if I wanted to achieve my goals.

We practiced this maneuver and others over and over to help rebuild my core muscles and balance. We even repeatedly went up and down curbs and slight hills, and got in and out of a simulated car. None of it was easy. And wearing the turtle brace made it extra hard.

At noon I rolled back to my room and closed the door. I didn't want anyone to see me discouraged.

Lunch arrived, giving me a chance to catch my breath and change my attitude. I needed to mentally prepare myself for my afternoon rehab session. But before I had time to regroup, there was a knock at the door.

"Come in," I said, just finishing my last bite of chicken salad.

"Hello, Dr. Wolf. I'm Dr. Steve Vangel, RIM's neuro-psychologist," he said with a smile, extending his hand. He had a firm handshake. I liked that. "May I sit down?" I nodded and motioned for him to sit next to me as I wiped my mouth with a napkin from my lunch tray. "I'd like to evaluate you for depression. Are you up for a few questions?" he asked, laying his tablet and pen on the table.

"No problem." As a physician, I was well aware of the effects a severe neurological trauma can have on some patients. Many require antidepressants as they try to adjust to their new reality. "What do you want to talk about?"

"My biggest question is, how are you coping with being paralyzed and in a wheelchair?"

"Well, I feel sad at times, and I get tired easily. It's a tough situation. I know this isn't going to be an easy road to travel. But I'm trying to stay positive."

"That's good," he affirmed. "How do you think being paralyzed will affect your marriage?"

"I'm not sure. My wife is a strong woman, though, and I know she's not going to leave me."

"You sound confident about that."

"I am."

"What about your sex life?"

"I've always enjoyed marital relations with my wife. But I know intercourse won't be possible anymore. So I'll have to find other ways to be intimate with her."

"I'm sure you'll figure it out."

Dr. Vangel continued to ask routine questions for about a half hour. But his final subject was the most difficult for me to talk about. "What's your greatest fear?"

"I don't want to lose my identity as a doctor and program director for my residents."

"I can understand that."

We shook hands again as he stood to leave.

"Your attitude and uncertainties appear to be normal, Dr. Wolf. I don't believe you need medication at this time. But I'm available to talk with you again if you have a need."

"Thank you. I'll be okay," I said, not knowing what the future had in store.

Occupational therapy began at one thirty. Diane, my OT, pushed me just as hard as Janine. She didn't cut me any slack. I had to practice dressing and undressing, and transferring to my shower chair and back.

In the middle of working on one of her assignments, I had a bowel movement. I felt completely humiliated. But Diane cleaned up the mess like it was no big deal. "I'm used to accidents," she said when she noticed the embarrassed look on my face. "This happens to all our patients, Dr. Wolf. You aren't the first, and you won't be the last."

At the moment, I couldn't have cared less how many other people experienced this. It was happening to me, and I was mortified.

Having soiled my pants, I needed to put on clean ones. I used the skills I'd just learned to transfer from my wheelchair onto a bed. That simple task almost totally depleted my energy.

Diane waited patiently. Once I was situated, she handed me a pair of sweatpants. "Here you go," she said with a smile.

Apparently she expected me to put them on by myself. Something most people took for granted. But I wasn't sure I could handle it.

"Come on, Dr. Wolf. You're tough. You can do this."

Obviously she had no intention of helping me. So I grunted, groaned, and sweated, with Diane cheering as she watched my contortions. She never rushed me or seemed discouraged with my slow progress.

When I finally got myself dressed, I had to get back into my wheelchair. Diane stood close by, ready to catch me if I lost my balance or started to fall. The challenge took my last ounce of strength, but I managed.

I welcomed returning to my room at the conclusion of the OT session. But there was still more rehab ahead of me that day.

Recreational therapy started at three thirty. I barely had enough strength to roll myself to the elevators and return to the main floor, where the sessions were held. But at least this type of therapy wouldn't be as physically demanding.

JC was the instructor for my first educational session. Three other patients were in the group. I felt uncomfortable in a class with other new paraplegics. I would have preferred a one-on-one with my new teacher.

First JC taught us about the importance of hygiene, which seemed like common sense to me. The next session explained our need to release pressure on the buttocks to prevent pressure ulcers from sitting in a wheelchair for long periods of time. She showed us how to raise ourselves up by placing our hands on the wheelchair armrests for support and then pushing up and holding for thirty seconds. I could only do it for five seconds the first time.

We were encouraged to get into the habit of doing this simple exercise every half hour. I understood the value of it. But it was difficult because I had so little strength.

After a strenuous day of rehab, I dreaded the thought of transferring back to my bed, knowing it would be a struggle because I was so physically and emotionally exhausted.

Back in my room, I convinced Keisha, my Patient Care Assistant, to help. She lifted me from my wheelchair until I could reach the trapeze bar above my bed. That provided enough momentum for me to swing myself onto the bed.

But my persuasive abilities provided only a temporary fix. I knew it would only delay my ability to transfer on my own—which I needed to do in order to lead an independent life.

The next day, I had a hard time breathing, and I passed out several times as a result of low blood pressure. Knowing I couldn't prevent this from happening was discouraging. To reduce the fainting spells, I was put in an abdominal binder to increase my blood pressure. It was terribly uncomfortable, and it added to the awkwardness of the turtle brace. But it was better than passing out.

A more embarrassing problem was my continued inability to control my bowels. I detested feeling so humiliated and dependent on others for help. But Keisha made my dignity a priority. When I pressed my call button, she arrived quickly, shut my door, and cleaned up my mess.

Keisha also provided extra attention when I showered. She was gentle and efficient as she removed my hospital gown, then made sure my genitals were covered with a towel before rolling me into the stall. After I finished, she covered me again before rolling me back to my bed. And she was patient as I struggled to get onto the bed.

Without my asking, she removed the wet turtle brace, dried it off, and put it back on me. She then assisted with getting me into my underwear. Next, she helped me put on my sweatpants, socks, shoes, and a clean abdominal binder. I managed to put on a fresh T-shirt myself.

Anita visited me that evening after work, and I told her about my strenuous day.

"I know this is difficult," she said. "But things will get better. You just need to accept your limitations without giving up your sense of independence. That will be a delicate balancing act for both of us, but we can do it!"

I liked hearing "we."

After Anita left, I felt more alone than ever. Dark emotions crept into my mind. *I don't know if I can make it. Am I going to end up a victim of my stupid mistake?* Giving up had never been a possibility for me—until then.

When I closed my eyes to try to sleep, a voice in my head said, *Pray, David. Pray.*

So I did. But these prayers were not my usual expressions of praise and gratitude for all the blessings in my life. My mind poured out frustrated, desperate thoughts.

God, you told me you were going to see me through this. You promise in your Word that you will pick me up when I fall and carry me when I can't go on. If you mean that, I need you to do it—now! Don't let me give up. Give me the strength and confidence to do better tomorrow.

I'm relying on you, Lord. I can't do this without you. I need your help to get me through. Forgive me for thinking I could do this by myself.

You are the Lord of my life. I love you, and I know you love me. Thank you for hearing my prayer and accepting my weaknesses. Amen.

Of course, I knew God would carry me. But he wanted me to humbly ask for his help. Turning my struggles over to him was an important step.

I finally prayed myself to sleep. As I slept, the promise of Hebrews 13:5 resonated in me: "Never will I leave you; never will I forsake you."

When morning came, I felt peace and acceptance. I knew without a doubt that God wouldn't leave me in despair or darkness.

I accepted the possibility that I might never walk again. But I was going to give it my best shot!

During my rehab workouts over the next few days, I had the strength of a mule. I transferred myself from my wheelchair and back again like I'd been doing it for a month.

God's grace and divine intervention got me through the first obstacle to recovery: believing I could climb this mountain by myself.

If you believe, you will receive whatever you ask for in prayer. MATTHEW 21:22

I was confident that prayer would get me through, that I could rely on God's help, and that he would transform my weaknesses if I allowed him to guide me. And yet I continued to wrestle with my greatest fear: losing my identity. I didn't want to stop being an OB/GYN physician just because I was disabled.

My fear was amplified when the chief of staff at Riverside Osteopathic Hospital came to my room with a document for my signature. It stated

I would relinquish my duties as chairman of the OB/GYN department until I could resume normal activities.

Numb with disbelief, I hesitated. But seeing no choice, I signed.

Later that day, the hospital CEO called with more bad news. "It is unlikely you'll be allowed to deliver babies or perform surgeries again."

My world seemed to be caving in. I loved being a doctor and couldn't imagine having my obstetric and surgical privileges taken away. I could handle my legs being paralyzed, but robbing me of my life's work? No way!

The phone rang again. More bad news?

"Hello?" I said in a dejected voice.

"Hey, Dave." It was my friend Dr. Sauter. "You sound down. Is something wrong?"

"You won't believe what happened today." I spilled my guts. "Can they do this to me?"

"Absolutely not." My normally laid-back friend sounded incensed. "I'm going to look into this!"

Moments after Bob's call, Dr. Nieshoff rolled into my room. I told him about the document and the CEO's phone call.

His eyes blazed. "You get that piece of paper and tear it up. Then tell those doctors to renege or we'll take them to court."

I clung to the thread of hope he dangled in front of me.

As a paralyzed physician, Dr. Nieshoff knew the laws and rights of disabled people. He had fought the disability war in his own life. His experience gave him confidence in the direction we needed to take.

I knew I was in good hands. His advice and assistance were a blessing from God.

The next day Dr. Nieshoff returned to my room with a big stack of research articles. "Send these to the hospital with a letter stating your position."

That afternoon, I dictated a letter to my office manager, Laurie. She typed it up, gave it to me to sign, then hand delivered it with the articles attached.

A few days later, I received a letter from the hospital stating there'd been a misunderstanding. The letter included a formal apology and a statement about "looking forward to your return."

I forgave the hospital executives, knowing they were just doing their jobs. But I was still hurt. Harboring anger and bitterness could have destroyed me. I was not about to let that happen.

> **Be kind and compassionate to one another, forgiving each other, just as in Christ God forgave you.** EPHESIANS 4:32

Somehow, *The Detroit News* got wind of my story and sent a reporter to interview Dr. Nieshoff and me along with other spinal-cord-injury patients for a news article. The headline read, "Cuts Hurt Paralysis Rehab." It addressed tragic facts related to the insurance and health-care industries concerning SCI patients. (See Appendix 2 for the full text of the article.)

I thanked God for bringing me wonderful men who went to bat for me.

> **I thank my God every time I remember you. In all my prayers for all of you, I always pray with joy because of your partnership in the gospel from the first day until now, being confident of this, that he who began a good work in you will carry it on to completion until the day of Christ Jesus.** PHILIPPIANS 1:3-6

As my rehab progressed, I asked Dr. Nieshoff numerous questions about my medical status. Almost every day, I requested to see my chart, and he always let me. It gave me a sense of control and kept me in the loop as a physician.

We had several lively conversations about my future. I was convinced I would walk again, even though he didn't believe it was possible.

At my request, Marc investigated standing wheelchair options. This device allows a paralyzed individual to raise the chair from a seated position to a standing position while being supported by leg and back safety straps. The chair can be operated manually or with a battery-powered hydraulic lift system. Some of the health benefits of a standing wheelchair include improved circulation, urinary health, bowel function, and bone density.

I believed having a standing wheelchair would give me a greater sense of independence and help me prepare for my return to work. The chairs were expensive, but I was willing to pursue the investment if it would allow me to continue doing surgeries until I was able to walk. So I purchased one and had it delivered to RIM. I thought it would be my ticket to mobility freedom.

When my office staff came to visit, I told them not to get used to seeing me in a wheelchair. "I'll be walking again in two years."

"I like your positive-thinking way of coping," Dr. Nieshoff said when he heard about my prediction. "It's a natural part of the grief process."

"What do you mean?"

"In many ways, becoming disabled is like experiencing a death in the family. You have to say good-bye to something precious: the way your body used to be. With time and perseverance you can learn to be happy again with yourself and your life."

Though I didn't waver in my belief that I would walk again, I appreciated his concern for me.

"David," he said, "disabled people can be healed . . . even when they can't be cured."

"I understand that," I assured him. "But I truly believe I will be cured."

My state of denial was evident to everyone but me.

13

Let's Go!

The harder you work,
the harder it is to surrender.
VINCE LOMBARDI

My routine in the rehab center was chaotic and frustrating. Early in the morning, my nursing attendant helped me transfer from the bed to the dual-purpose shower-and-commode chair. It was a clumsy and tiring process due to my cumbersome turtle brace. And I never got used to disrobing in front of her. Unlike Keisha, this woman did not cover me with a towel to make the situation less awkward.

The small wheels prevented me from moving myself, so my attendant had to push me to the shower. Fortunately, she left me to clean up on my own. It took longer than usual because I was confined to the turtle brace and had to use a handheld showerhead.

Afterward, I pulled the emergency cord. The attendant returned to help me dry off. It was embarrassing.

Then she pushed me to the sink, where she left me alone to shave. Holding my arms up was tiring. Several times I had to take a break and rest a few moments. This routine task took about fifteen minutes longer than before my accident.

After doing the best job on my beard that I could, I waited for the attendant to return. There was no emergency cord, like there was in the shower. So I had no choice but to sit there.

Two hours later, I was still sitting in the bathroom, waiting for the attendant.

Did she forget me? I considered screaming, just to see if someone would respond. But I didn't.

Finally, the attendant showed up. I told her this time lapse was inexcusable. She shrugged, not even offering an explanation, much less an apology.

The same thing happened several days in a row. One time, I sat in the bathroom waiting so long, my low blood pressure caused me to faint. The attendant eventually returned and got me back to my bed.

"Something has to be done about this," I complained to Anita when she came to see me.

She agreed. And she came up with a great idea.

The next day she returned with my English bulldog's leash. She attached one end to the shower cord and looped the red leather handle around my can of shaving cream, making it easy to pull the cord. A perfect solution!

I used the makeshift device to call the attendant as soon as I finished shaving the next time.

"How did you pull the cord?" she asked, her eyes wide.

"I rigged it," I said smugly.

It felt good to have some control. Even this small thing made a big difference.

The following Sunday afternoon, three of my colleagues came to see me: Dr. Ronald Ayres, Dr. Ronald Librizzi, and Dr. Joseph Bonanno. Each had a thriving medical practice and was on the executive committee of the American Osteopathic Board of Obstetrics and Gynecology, the certifying board for osteopathic OB/GYN physicians. They had flown in from Philadelphia and Chicago just to visit me.

Since I was the chairman of the clinical examination committee, I tried carrying on a conversation about the certifying board. But they wanted to talk about how I was feeling and progressing.

For a moment, I was caught off guard. But when I got over my shock, I talked openly with them. What a joy to know their visit was more than a professional courtesy.

Before leaving, they gave me a gift: a laptop computer. At the time, I wasn't into computers. But I learned quickly. This technology was a challenge, but it provided me with a new way to communicate.

Their presence—and their kind and thoughtful gift—meant a great deal to me. I felt on top of the world when they left.

But the day got even better.

That afternoon, several nurses and other professional staff from the Labor and Delivery Department at Riverside Osteopathic Hospital came to visit me. We laughed and joked, sharing our L&D stories. I surprised them with my exuberant spirit.

Friends and colleagues made a big difference in my progress just by being there. Each visitor gave me a boost, adding to my strength and determination to achieve my goals.

Their visits may have seemed like a small thing to them, but it was a huge blessing to me. Friendship and time are priceless gifts.

The next day, my daughter, Raquel, skipped school to visit me. Giving up a day when you're working on your master's degree is a generous gift!

I was in an occupational therapy group session, learning how to adjust to everyday activities at home, when she popped her head in the door, grinning from ear to ear. My heart soared when I saw her. I didn't hear another word the therapist said.

Raquel wanted to help with my therapy tasks. So we practiced getting me in and out of a simulated car. She almost dropped me a couple of times. We laughed as we struggled to accomplish this task—so crucial to my progress, yet comical to observe.

I wanted to show off my progress, so I let her watch me try to put on my pants. I was determined to succeed, despite wearing the turtle brace. Sweat rolled down my face.

"Come on, Dad. You can do it! You still want to wear the pants in the family, right?" she joked.

Ha! You try doing this with a dumb brace, I thought. But I managed to smile—and achieve my goal.

Raquel's encouragement made a crucial difference in my attitude. Her cheerleading gave me the drive I needed to press on.

The people who came alongside me during this time helped me to understand how God uses others to help us accomplish our goals. I could no more win in my rehabilitation regime without my support team than I could have excelled in my go-kart racing without my mechanics.

My recreational therapist, JC, insisted I build up my strength by rolling my wheelchair through the two-city-blocks-long tunnel system of the medical complex. Some days, she and I would go outside and roll over to Wendy's for lunch. The late-summer sun felt good. The fast-food goal motivated me, especially since I got hungry after a good workout.

We also practiced going up and down ramps and rolling the wheelchair on the grass. Sometimes JC pushed if I needed a break. It was tough, but I loved working hard. I was up for the challenge!

JC and I became good friends during my four in-patient (and increasingly impatient!) weeks. I enjoyed the meaningful conversations we shared. Most of the medical team merely asked, "How are you today, Doctor?" I appreciated their concern. But JC went beyond that. She provided me with a lot of insight. And she was one of the first people to suggest I write a book.

She always went out of her way for me. To her, it was a little thing. To me, it was huge.

I was fortunate to have been given many gifts of love, friendship, and encouragement in my life. I had Jesus in my heart. Plus, I had the financial resources to get a better life after rehab.

I knew, sadly, that others around me weren't as blessed.

Several wives came to see their husbands, but they soon realized that a permanently paralyzed husband presented a gloomy future and a tremendous commitment. Some wives didn't want to live like that, so they would leave and not come back. This resulted in depression for many of the men, who felt abandoned. With nowhere else to go, some resigned themselves to life in a nursing home. How tragic.

I became passionate about their situation and resolved to be their advocate. I felt God had placed me there to help.

One time when I overheard a guy talk about having to go to a nursing home, I said, "Get that thought out of your mind. We're going to talk to the social worker about this."

I took him to the social worker and explained the situation. But since this guy didn't have anyone to help him at home, she said, "Sorry, but this is the best we can do for him."

"No way," I argued. "He doesn't have to go to a nursing home. You can keep him here until he can function on his own. Just make him work harder."

That meant the rehab team had to work harder too. But everyone pulled together to make it happen.

Whenever I attended a therapy session, I started noticing if someone was missing. Without a second thought, I'd find the guy's room and get right in his face.

"Hey, man, why aren't you in rehab?" I'd ask.

"I don't feel like going down today, Dr. Wolf."

"What do you mean? If I'm going, you're going. Now, get out of that bed and come with me. You'll feel better later if you do."

I refused to take no for an answer. Before long, these guys started coming down more often to work out. It was easier than being harassed by me! They even stayed after the scheduled workout time to lift weights on their own, which was something I did every day. I loved watching their attitudes change.

JC asked me to teach the "Taking Care of Yourself" class. She felt that patients would be more attentive if they heard the information from someone in their shoes. Plus, she knew I really enjoyed teaching.

The atmosphere at RIM seemed to improve while I was there. It may have been only temporary, but I think my attitude made a difference and rubbed off on others. Motivating people filled me with energy.

We were all struggling, all hoping for a better life. The difference was, I knew God's love and strength. I couldn't let anyone give up. So I became their coach. My presence there had purpose. That was great medicine—for them and for me!

My command is this: Love each other as I have loved you.
JOHN 15:12

Unexpected blessings kept flowing as I asked God for his guidance and direction. As I strived to provide some small benefit for others, they were a huge benefit to me.

The need to express my gratitude became a priority. I felt compelled to say thank you for every card, phone call, or personal visit. So I dictated letters for Laurie to type. She arranged for a small filing cabinet to be placed in my room so I could keep all my correspondence there.

Every morning I'd wake up and see the filing cabinet next to my wheelchair. I focused on that filing cabinet. It became a symbol of hope. But the possibility of losing my identity kept haunting me.

Upon waking early one morning, an idea occurred to me about contacting *The News-Herald* to get my story printed in the paper. I wanted people to know how determined I was to still be an OB/GYN physician.

I knew the editor personally. Fred Manuel attended the same church I did. His kids and ours used to play together.

When I called, he was interested but direct. "If we print your story as you're suggesting, it's going to cost several thousand dollars. But if you let us interview you as a human-interest story for our readers, it won't cost anything."

That sounded good to me.

"There's just one catch. You won't be able to edit what we write. It'll be our decision what to include or not include."

"I want people to know about my faith in God and my determination to return to work," I said.

He couldn't make any guarantees. But I accepted his offer anyway.

My story was published on August 22, 2001, barely three weeks after the go-kart racing accident. The headline read, "Doctor Learns to Live as Patient after Ohio Go-Kart Mishap." The article highlighted my accident and my hopes of returning to OB/GYN medicine. (See Appendix 3 for the full text of this article.) It was a good piece, but I was disappointed that my personal beliefs weren't mentioned.

"If you want your feelings heard, you should write a letter to the community," Fred said when I told him of my disappointment. "It won't take up much space to be published, so it won't cost much."

His advice made sense. So I wrote the letter. My goal was to accomplish two things. First, I wanted to acknowledge the people who'd prayed for me or called with expressions of care and encouragement. Second, I wanted people to know this was not the end of Dr. Wolf. I was definitely coming back!

My letter, "A Heartfelt Thank-You from Dr. David Wolf," appeared in the first section of the Sunday paper twice: September 2 and September 9. I was excited, because more people read (or at least glance at) the Sunday newspaper than any other edition. (See Appendix 4 to read this letter.)

Throughout the challenges of my recovery, my wife stood by my side, quietly enduring every step of this life-changing experience with her calm strength. Her loyalty and commitment to our wedding vows has been unwavering.

Anita has a pure heart, filled with the Holy Spirit. Her faith and unceasing prayers are immeasurable gifts. By seeking God's strength and guidance, one day at a time, she has maintained a confident presence. Anita was and still is my rock!

Trust in the Lord with all your heart and lean not on your own understanding; in all your ways acknowledge him, and he will make your paths straight. PROVERBS 3:5–6

Anita's spiritual focus enabled her to make practical decisions and communicate sensibly. With an upbeat, positive tone, she continually reminded me about the importance of accepting my limitations and new means of mobility. Yet she was relentless in doing everything possible to prevent me from becoming too dependent on her.

Ironically, she received less of my thanks and appreciation than the others. I just expected her to be there.

I'm embarrassed to admit, Anita often became the recipient of my frustrations with myself. She didn't deserve that, but she absorbed it with dignity and grace. Only a wise woman could rely on God's love during such times of inequity.

Her focus is on the Lord, not herself. She humbly serves him.

After the suffering of his soul, he will see the light of life and be satisfied; by his knowledge my righteous servant will justify many, and he will bear their iniquities. Isaiah 53:11

14

Shocking Change, Fragile Emotions

There are no mistakes, no coincidences.
All events are blessings given to us to learn from.
ELIZABETH KÜBLER-ROSS

L imited time with Anita at RIM wasn't what I would have preferred. But I understood her time constraints as she focused on preparations for my homecoming. This huge task involved addressing many concerns.

Fortunately, we had decided to sell our large tri-level home several months before my accident. Downsizing had seemed realistic since Brad and Raquel lived in their own places. We'd agreed to buy a condominium that was half the size of our current home and knew the general location we wanted. We were ready for a change.

God had been preparing us for our new life even before we knew we'd have one. Having to make that kind of decision after my accident would have added an extra burden to the difficult situation.

A one-story residence was practical for handicap accessibility. Less than a week after my accident, a ground-floor condo in a perfect area became available. Some people may call it a coincidence, but I don't believe in coincidences.

Getting the condo ready for my arrival was no easy task. After work and on the weekends Anita spent hours with home-improvement vendors looking at flooring surfaces, bathroom fixtures, paint colors, and more. Additionally, she had to make arrangements with a moving company to pack and move our belongings.

She concentrated on making my transition to our new home as easy and pleasant as possible. She had hardwood floors and low-pile carpet installed for easier maneuvering of my wheelchair. And she had the doors to our bedroom and my study removed so my wheelchair could fit through the doorway.

She also hired Frank to redesign the bathroom. He built a roll-in shower with a handheld unit. He also installed higher cabinets and sink, and a new toilet. The new bathroom was completely handicap accessible.

All of this was accomplished during the four weeks I was at RIM.

Anita kept me involved by providing daily updates on the project. She asked for my input on room design and decorating plans, knowing I would feel valued by being included in some of the decisions.

As the last week of rehab approached, my physical strength and coordination had improved, but my emotional condition was still fragile. I felt discouraged because my bowels and fainting spells were still issues and I was tired a lot of the time. Fear of not knowing how I'd handle my new lifestyle crept into my thoughts daily.

I did my best to stay focused on my immediate goal: to be discharged in time to attend the Notre Dame game and watch them stomp Purdue! I discussed this with Anita, and we made plans to go directly from RIM to our lake home in Monticello, Indiana, that Friday, then drive to the stadium from there on Saturday. September 15—what a great day it promised to be!

Tragically, four days before the game, the world stopped in shock at the horrific attack on the Twin Towers. Extreme measures were immediately taken to heighten the nation's security efforts.

Like many Americans, I sat glued to the TV, watching the sickening and unimaginable story unfold throughout the day.

The day before my scheduled release from RIM, Anita broke the news to me that the Notre Dame–Purdue game had been cancelled. "It's probably for the best," she said calmly. "A big trip to the lake house and then the game would've been very strenuous. And going from no social activity to a full weekend would have been a huge undertaking."

I knew she was right. Our lake home hadn't been made handicap accessible yet. And the five-hour drive home would have been difficult with me wearing the turtle brace.

Cancellation of the game was a relief for Anita. But to me, it meant another hope being dashed. I felt so crushed I was on the verge of crying like a child when a favorite toy gets broken.

Later that night Raquel called. She understood how I felt and had a solution to the problem. "Dad, we're still taking you to Indiana tomorrow," she said optimistically. "We'll go to Purdue to watch a scrimmage." Purdue is where Raquel completed her undergraduate studies. "You won't see Notre Dame, but we'll all be together: you, me, and Mom. Grandma will be at the lake waiting for us afterward."

I was deeply touched and comforted. Having something to look forward to settled my emotions. At least we'd be at the same stadium.

Yet I wondered what it would be like seeing my mom for the first time since my accident. We had talked on several occasions during my hospital stay and my rehab at RIM. But seeing her face-to-face would be a different matter.

Preparing to leave RIM had its emotional consequences. I couldn't bear the thought that I might never see these new friends again. I'd become dependent on others and comfortable with my rehab plateau.

I loved my RIM family. They accepted me and encouraged me to never give up on my dreams. We had laughed, cried, shared pieces of our lives, and learned from one another. I received more than excellent medical care from them. They also gave me food for my spirit.

Tears of gratitude flowed when I said my final good-byes.

Keep on loving each other as brothers. HEBREWS 13:1

15

Charting New Territory

Just as parents delight in the talk of their children,
so God delights when we talk to him in prayer.

BILLY GRAHAM

RIM gave me a transfer board to sit on when I needed to get in and out of the car. Its smooth, varnished wood surface would help me accomplish the task with less difficulty. Anita and I practiced using it twice during my therapy. She felt confident we could manage the process by ourselves.

Our skills were put to the test when we left for our lake home. I wheeled up to the passenger side of the car, opened the door, swung the left arm of my wheelchair out of the way, positioned myself flush with the car seat, and locked the wheelchair in place. After Anita handed me the twenty-four-by-eight-inch board, I put it on the seat as close to the wheelchair as possible. Then I lifted my left leg into the car, positioned my left hand and upper body weight on the board, and scooted myself onto the seat. Anita held the wheelchair tightly to prevent it from slipping. Once I was situated, she lifted my right leg into the car. We were exhausted even before our adventure began!

Mixed emotions filled my heart and mind during the five-hour drive to Monticello, Indiana. I felt sad leaving my RIM friends, but happy to be going to the place where my family had gathered together so many times over the years for special occasions. It's where we've always gone to relax and take a break from our busy lives.

THE GIFT IS YOU

The drive was uncomfortable and tiring. Being confined to the turtle brace made the trip especially difficult. But at least we were more prepared to use the transfer board when we arrived.

While Anita removed my wheelchair from the trunk, I opened the passenger door and waited for her to roll the chair to me. Desperately wanting to do whatever I could, I scooted to the edge of the car seat, took a deep breath, and awkwardly lifted myself onto the wheelchair. Anita spotted, in case I lost my balance. It took all my strength and ten minutes of teamwork to do this task. But we did it!

I rolled up the driveway onto the sidewalk to the back of the house. Anita walked behind me. I couldn't navigate the porch by myself, so she tilted me backward, lifting me onto it.

When she opened the door and I gazed at the familiar surroundings, a sense of peace covered me.

Mom was seated on the living room couch. As we entered, she looked up and saw me in a wheelchair for the first time. Hands folded tightly in her lap, she stared intently. Tears flooded her eyes.

I rolled over and gave her a hug. She wrapped her arms around me and burst into tears. "I can't believe God would do this to you." I seldom saw her cry, but I wasn't surprised at the outburst.

Her tears soaked the shoulder of my shirt while I patted her gently on the back. "I did this to myself. It was my misguided obsession for racing go-karts that put me here."

Tears continued to stream down her face as I searched for the right words to say.

"And I'm okay. I can't move my legs, but I'm the same person I've always been, and I don't want you to think of me differently."

She wiped the tears from her cheeks. "I know, David. I've been praying a lot. And I do trust God to see you through this. It's just not easy for me, seeing you like this."

I smiled confidently. "It's not the end of the world, Mom. Great things are going to happen in this wheelchair. See, God talked to me while I was in the hospital. He said he would take care of me and that he has a new mission for my life."

She closed her eyes for a moment, then kissed me on the cheek. I

knew that was her way of showing me that she believed in me.

Raquel's weekend plan worked out great. Attending the Purdue scrimmage was exciting, even though it wasn't our annual football game tradition. And being at the lake with family was pure joy. But I didn't look forward to the tiring and uncomfortable five-hour drive back to Michigan.

Once we were on the road to our new residence, I couldn't hush the voices that ran rampant through my mind.

Can I be happy living in the condo in my wheelchair?

Will my faith be strong enough to help me adjust to my new lifestyle?

Will Anita be able to survive this new life?

Can we learn to live together 24/7? Prior to the accident, I worked long hours, so our time together had been limited.

All of these unknowns taunted me. I struggled with not knowing what the future held.

When we finally got home, I had to admit that Anita was right—as usual. Even with the abridged schedule, my first family weekend had taken its toll. We were both completely worn out. But I made it through—by the grace of God and my awesome wife!

> He said to me, "My grace is sufficient for you, for my power is made perfect in weakness." 2 CORINTHIANS 12:9

When we arrived at our new home, getting me out of the car was easier than the first time since we knew what to expect.

The condo was small in comparison to our family home. But it had an open concept and didn't feel crowded. Everything was neat and put away when I entered. Anita and a few of her friends had worked long hours to prepare for my arrival.

I liked the hardwood floors in the entrance and hallway, making it easy to get around in the wheelchair. I rolled into my favorite room, the study, and took in the sight of familiar items from my previous study: my credenza, the tall shelf stocked with my favorite books, and framed photos of the kids and memories with friends.

The vaulted ceiling provided a wall large enough to hold my favorite piece of art: an original abstract of a seated pregnant woman, painted by a Florida artist. The fifty-eight-by-seventy-inch canvas took up a major portion of the wall. On the opposite wall hung a framed photo of a Notre Dame helmet held high by a fist, symbolizing victory.

My oversized desk stood in the middle of the room. Frank had raised it to accommodate my wheelchair. I rolled up to it and felt comfortable with the new height.

The living room contained most of the furniture from the old house. One of the few pieces that mattered to me was my black leather reclining chair. I would have more time to enjoy it now than before my accident. My first try at transferring to and from the recliner was a challenge. But I transferred by myself!

The bedroom looked like it belonged to someone else. Anita had been emotionally attached to our bedroom furniture because it had been passed down from her grandmother to her mother and then given to her. But since it was too high for me to use, we'd sold it. The new bed was level with my wheelchair seat. A special air mattress, provided by RIM to prevent pressure sores, was on the metal frame. The shower chair we'd recently purchased sat next to the dresser.

In spite of the unfamiliar feeling of the room, my body ached to end the long day. Unfortunately, bedtime was an ordeal. I took off my own shirt, but Anita had to help me undress from the waist down. Gripping the arms of my wheelchair with both hands, I lifted my lower body and held the position while Anita pulled off my pants and elastic thigh-high support socks. Noticing my arms start to quiver, she moved quickly.

Getting me onto the bed was next. I swung the right arm of the wheel-chair away and positioned the chair as close as possible to the side of the bed, then locked it down. After placing my right hand firmly on the bed, I lifted and pivoted myself onto it in one motion. After my bottom was in place, I put both hands on the bed for balance. Anita strained to lift the dead weight of my paralyzed legs onto the bed. But she didn't complain once.

The third step was to remove the turtle brace. Supported by my elbows,

I leaned back and rolled to my right side. Anita removed the back of the turtle brace, then helped me roll onto my back to remove the front piece.

Once the turtle brace was off, she wedged a pillow under my back so I could sleep on my right side. Then she put a body pillow between my legs and feet to help prevent pressure sores.

The entire routine took twenty minutes. It took all my strength and all of Anita's as well.

When we finally lay down together, we looked at each other in dismay. "I've set the alarm clock for two a.m." Anita sighed. RIM had instructed her to turn me every four hours during the night, an added precaution against wounds developing. "I think we'll need to be up by six to start the morning routine. Okay?"

I nodded, speechless.

Simple tasks we'd taken for granted in the past were going to take a lot longer and require far more determination than I had imagined possible. Would we ever get a good night's sleep again? Or would this new routine drive both of us crazy?

Before sinking into a deep sleep, I silently thanked God for Anita and prayed for his continued help for both of us.

The Lord gives strength to his people; the Lord blesses his people with peace. PSALM 29:11

Anita got up as soon as the six o'clock alarm went off. She went outside to get the morning paper, but it had not been delivered at the usual six o'clock time. I'd always performed this small task. Yet another responsibility had been added to her routine.

She returned to the bedroom with a smile. "Good morning!" she said in a cheery voice.

"Good morning," I said out of courtesy. But I didn't smile.

I felt helpless as Anita removed my underwear and put me back in my turtle brace prison. Once the Velcro straps were secured, she raised my shoulders while I pushed myself up to a sitting position. Then she rolled the shower chair to the side of the bed and held it firmly while I lifted myself onto the open seat.

The large rubber tires rolled easily on the hardwood floor as I got myself into the bathroom and positioned myself over the toilet. I liked having the independence to begin my hygiene schedule without help.

I reached for the newspaper, suddenly realizing it still had not been delivered and placed on the counter by Anita. Since my accident, reading the articles helped me relax so I could have a bowel movement. But this normal bodily function took even more time because I was tense and couldn't feel anything.

The shower area had been designed specifically for me. I'd always looked forward to the simple pleasure of a hot shower every morning. But the turtle brace made soaping up my entire body impossible.

After getting myself as clean as I could, I grabbed a towel off the low bar and dried my head, arms, and upper legs. I'd have to wait till Anita removed the turtle brace before drying the rest of my body. While I was in there, I shaved.

The entire bathroom regime took over an hour. During that time Anita dressed for the day and laid out my clean clothes.

I got back in bed to have the turtle brace removed. Anita helped dry my back and my feet. Then we put the turtle brace back on.

Putting my clothes on took more strength and time than taking them off. I could slip on a T-shirt by myself, but Anita had to help with my underwear, pants, stockings, and shoes. I felt like a helpless infant while she maneuvered my legs on the bed. I did my best to help but could only use my arms to raise my hips.

Our faces were damp with perspiration by the time I was fully dressed. "This awkward routine has taken two hours already, and there's still more to do," I said, frustrated.

The last task was getting me back into the wheelchair. It took pure determination on both our parts.

I glanced at the bedside clock. It was almost eight thirty. "You have to leave now if you're going to make it to work on time."

She checked her watch. "You're right." She hurried to the kitchen. I followed her in my wheelchair. In one quick motion she scooped up her car keys and purse off the counter, then turned back to kiss me good-bye. "I wish I didn't have to go," she said, tearing up.

"I'll be all right." I hoped I sounded more confident than I felt.

"Coffee's ready. Call if you need me."

I nodded. "Be safe."

My heart pounded when I heard the SUV engine start. I rolled to my study and watched out the window as she drove away. Tears clung to my cheeks while I sat in silence with my internal darkness.

Anita had to maintain her work schedule at the hospital. We needed her income, especially during the waiting period before we started receiving insurance benefits from my accident. But for the past month and a half, I'd never been completely alone. Someone had always been available to help me if needed. Now I was on my own. And that frightened me.

Loneliness hit me hard as I wheeled through the silent house. The rush of my overscheduled life had ceased. I had to face a new reality—again.

What am I going to do all day?

I couldn't drive. We'd made plans to purchase a handicapped van but that had not been done yet.

I couldn't go to work. I couldn't see patients. I couldn't see my residents at the hospital.

I couldn't call my friends. They were all at work.

I considered reading books, but I couldn't do that all day. And daytime TV didn't interest me at all.

I couldn't even go to outpatient therapy until the turtle brace came off. That wouldn't happen for eight more weeks.

I hated that brace!

Anita had mentioned coffee. Deciding to get some, I rolled to the kitchen. The fresh-brewed aroma filled my nostrils. But to my disappointment, Anita had forgotten to put a mug next to the pot. I couldn't reach the mugs in the cabinet. I couldn't reach the toaster or the bread and peanut butter in the pantry, either.

I still had a lot to learn about living in a wheelchair.

When I heard a thunking sound outside, I wheeled back to my study. Looking out the window, I saw a rolled-up newspaper on the sidewalk near our mailbox. I was relieved it had finally arrived. Frantic for something to occupy my lonely hours, I hurried to the front door, grateful that Anita had arranged for delivery to our new home. After some awkward maneuvering, I managed to open the door.

I gazed longingly at the newspaper lying a few feet past our tiny porch. There was just one obstacle between me and that precious link to the outside world: an eight-inch concrete step.

I recalled Anita asking if I thought we should install a ramp on the front porch. But I didn't want to advertise to our new neighbors that I was handicapped.

Now, because of my foolish pride, I couldn't get the newspaper—or the mail.

I'd never felt so isolated.

Buster Brown, my English bulldog, and Taffy, my golden retriever, sensed my sadness and followed me from one room to another. When I finally settled in the living room for a few minutes, they both lay next to the wheelchair. After a few minutes, Taffy stood and looked up at me, as if to say, *You'll feel better if you pet me.*

"Okay, Taffy," I said, stroking her head. "You're a good girl."

The arduous morning routine and negative emotions had depleted my energy. But I forced myself to transfer to my Lazy Boy recliner. It took all my strength. When I'd finally settled in, I stretched out. Exhaustion took over. In the middle of a prayer asking God to help me not be afraid and not give up, I fell asleep.

Take courage! It is I. Don't be afraid. Matthew 14:27

The sound of the automatic garage door opening cheered me up. Seeing Anita come into the house was like watching an angel appear.

"I'm so glad you're back," I groaned. "It's been lonely around here all by myself. Now I have somebody to talk to."

She hurried to my side and kissed my forehead. "I'm sorry. I don't like having to be away. It was really tough leaving here this morning, knowing you need me."

My whining didn't help her frustration. I had to try to keep my grumbling to myself so as not to make her feel worse.

Before getting dinner ready, Anita helped me focus by sharing some meaningful and timely Bible passages she'd discovered.

One of my favorites was Philippians 4:6: "Do not be anxious about anything, but in everything, by prayer and petition, with thanksgiving, present your requests to God." This verse reminded me to rely on God as he nudged me along my new path.

About two weeks after moving into our new home, Anita was off work on Saturday. "I've got some errands to run," she told me. "But I'll be back before dinner."

"No problem," I said calmly. I didn't mind her leaving for a couple of hours. It'd give me a chance to start organizing my thoughts for the new certifying board exam. "I'll probably be at my desk when you get home."

After Anita left I rolled into my study with a sense of purpose. I felt comfortable sitting behind my familiar desk. I'd made many plans and done scores of paperwork there. And having a goal to focus on helped lessen my loneliness.

After locking myself in place, I took a large yellow tablet from the drawer and picked up a pen. As I started to write, I realized my wheelchair was too close to the desk. Still holding the pen, I unlocked the wheels to push myself back a bit. The pen slipped out of my fingers and landed on the hardwood floor. I leaned forward to pick up the pen, lost my balance, and fell forward, landing face-first on the floor. The wheelchair slammed against the wall behind the desk.

I lay there, stunned.

As I assessed my situation, I realized that the turtle brace had broken my fall, preventing further injury to my back. It was the one time I was glad to be wearing it.

Regrettably, I couldn't get back into the wheelchair. The turtle brace restricted me from bending my torso. And without the aid of my core muscles, my arms didn't have enough strength to lift my body.

I decided to play it safe and roll from one side to the other every fifteen minutes. At least that would give me something to do while waiting for Anita's return. Unfortunately, the only clock in the room was on my desk. But I couldn't just lie there until Anita came home. RIM hadn't told me how long it took for pressure sores to develop on hard surfaces.

With tremendous effort, I managed to roll onto my side. My quivering muscles resisted gravity's power enough to pull myself up to the edge of the desk.

Immediately I noticed my cell phone. It was within my reach. But if I called Anita or 911, I'd be admitting I couldn't take care of myself. I didn't want anyone, not even my wife, to think I was weak.

Holding on with all my might, I stretched one arm across the desk and grabbed the small digital clock. Then I used my other hand to slowly lower myself back to the floor.

I lay there, sweating and panting, too exhausted to move a muscle.

When I finally caught my breath, I checked the time. It was two o'clock. I could lie on the hardwood floor till two fifteen before trying to roll over.

Seeing my soft leather briefcase next to the desk, I pulled it across the floor and positioned it like a pillow to support my neck.

The minutes dragged by. My eyelids became too heavy to keep watching the red digits on the clock change.

Finally I surrendered. As I drifted off to sleep, I prayed. "Lord, I'm in trouble. If my friends could see me now, they wouldn't see a very godly attitude. Please forgive me for being such a prideful man."

My eyes sprang open at the sound of Anita's voice yelling my name. I glanced at the clock. An hour had passed.

"What happened?" She rushed to my side, her eyes wide with fear.

"I'm okay. I was reaching for a pen I dropped and fell out of my chair."

As soon as she knew I was all right, her tense shoulders relaxed. After helping me back into my chair, she picked up the alarm clock off the floor. "Why is this down here?"

"I wanted to roll over every fifteen minutes, to prevent pressure sores." That plan hadn't worked. I wondered how much damage I'd done by lying still on the hard floor for an hour.

Anita put the clock back on the desk. "So you managed to pull yourself up to the desk . . . but you didn't grab the phone?" She put her hands on her hips. "Why didn't you call 911? Or me?"

"I didn't want to bother you."

She maneuvered the wheelchair next to my body as she continued to reprimand me. "You could have at least called Frank. He would have come over and put you back in your wheelchair. I left the door unlocked."

"You're right. I'm sorry." But it hadn't even occurred to me to call Frank.

I felt ashamed as we struggled to get me back in the chair.

Anita left me sitting at my desk. I watched her walk down the hall. I knew she was still upset because I could hear her on the phone in another room venting to Raquel.

Later that day, Raquel called. "Dad," she scolded, "you've got to start using that big brain of yours or people will start thinking you're stupid!"

My daughter's words bothered me. I didn't want anyone to consider me stupid. "You're right. I'm sorry." The same words I'd told Anita.

Not long after my talk with Raquel, Brad called. "You know, Dad, if you don't stop this nonsense, Mom's going to end up in the hospital." Obviously, Anita had told him about my embarrassing incident too.

His words pierced my heart and cut deep. My pride could have caused a worse situation. "I'm sorry," I repeated, regretting my foolish decision.

A man's pride brings him low, but a man of lowly spirit gains honor. PROVERBS 29:23

For the rest of the day I contemplated my earlier behavior. Something had to change. Going from being overscheduled to having no schedule at all had created an emotional roller coaster for me. I had to find a way to control my feelings and make sound decisions.

I knew that staying rooted in God was my only salvation. Without reassurance of his love and his presence, I could easily fall prey to a self-defeating, prideful attitude.

So I prayed diligently, day and night.

Lord, please give me stability and guidance. I know you will see me through even the worst of times. Thank you for figuring this thing out and working on positive outcomes for my future. In Jesus' name I pray. Amen.

As I spent time in God's presence, the tidal wave of worry slowly subsided. I began to feel less isolated. I actually started appreciating my alone times because I could pray out loud any time I wanted to without distractions.

During those times of solitude, the Lord penetrated my heart with his voice. He used this tough situation to change my competitive personality and workaholic behavior.

> **God did not give us a spirit of timidity, but a spirit of power, of love and of self-discipline.** 2 TIMOTHY 1:7

God was using my circumstances to teach me about the importance of having a close relationship with him. What mattered most was talking with him—and listening to him.

As I began taking a moment to think before doing things, my awareness of situations improved and I started becoming more resourceful. For example, I had Anita purchase a hand-grabber tool for me to use when I needed to reach something higher or lower than the restrictions of my wheelchair would allow.

I prayed every day for God to guide me by the Holy Spirit in my thoughts, words, and actions. As I listened more closely to his direction, I learned that physical vulnerability is not the same as weak character and the processes of independence and interdependence are not incompatible.

> **Jesus said, "He who has ears to hear, let him hear."** MARK 4:9

Challenges continued as I learned to navigate with limited mobility. But figuring out new ways of doing things became a normal part of day-to-day living.

God knew my competitive personality and my desire to do things my way. But these issues did not hold me back from his mission for my life. My confidence remained steadfast. My body may have been in a wheelchair, but my head and heart were not.

When friends came to visit, they couldn't believe I was not depressed. Some thought I was in denial about my situation. But most saw the amazing trust that shone brighter and brighter with every God-given event in my life. They knew the twinkle in my eye was only because of him.

16

Shot of Confidence

Destiny is no matter of chance. It is a matter of choice.
It is not a thing to be waited for; it is a thing to be achieved.
WILLIAM JENNINGS BRYAN

One of the biggest and most unexpected challenges in the beginning of my new journey was learning how to deal with undignified treatment from people who didn't know me.

Strangers laughed at me. (At least it seemed so to me.) Glances and stares were not uncommon. Some faces had a look of pity. I'd never been viewed with pity before.

Hey, people, give me a break! I'm the same person I've always been, except for this wheelchair ... I think. I wondered why people were so insensitive.

Some folks acted like I was deaf, dumb, and blind. They only addressed Anita when we were together.

At one restaurant, Anita and I were seated in the back, out of the way. The waitress asked my wife what I wanted to eat. Even worse, she gave *her* the bill. Add *invisible* to the list.

When it was time to leave that restaurant, since our table was in the back, other diners had to get up and move their chairs so we could get out. The whole situation seemed very demeaning.

"I'm never going back to that place," I grumbled as we crossed the parking lot.

"Oh, yes, you are," Anita insisted. "I'm going back, and you're going with me."

My lovely wife would not let me give up. She loved me through times of frustration, discouragement, and loneliness. And she never complained about her added responsibilities or my moodiness.

Together, by the grace of God, we made it through my darkest days. The mercy and light of Jesus held me up through my wife's kindness, perseverance, and unwavering commitment to our marriage and, even more important, to the Lord.

> **Do not let any unwholesome talk come out of your mouths, but only what is helpful for building others up according to their needs, that it may benefit those who listen.**
> Ephesians 4:29

Every day brought new experiences that continually reminded me of my paralysis. Neighbors would be walking by and I'd wave as Anita and I pulled out of the driveway, unable to join them. People at church would be mingling in the foyer after service and I'd have to sit in one place, waiting for someone to come to me for a conversation. I'd see colleagues at a restaurant, and they talked about a recent out-of-town conference they'd attended. Their mobility and independence always triggered strong emotions about my new life. But I never lost sight of my goal to return to my medical practice and be a successful OB/GYN physician again.

I remained in constant prayer to ensure I would not be held captive by frustration, dignity issues, and an uncertain future. Faith in God's plan for my life provided the strength necessary to carry on each day. I wanted my new mission to be an authentic testimony to glorify God. I had to "walk the talk."

> **I consider that our present sufferings are not worth comparing with the glory that will be revealed in us.** Romans 8:18

The luxury of free time was new to me, but I took advantage of it. As chairman of the Clinical Examination Committee for the American Osteopathic Board of Obstetrics and Gynecology, I focused my energy on developing a better oral certifying exam for the OB/GYN physicians.

It was something I'd wanted to do for a long time, but carving out extra hours had been nearly impossible before my accident. This project gave me something to look forward to each day.

The new exam was scheduled to be presented at a meeting in Chicago in late October, barely a month after I arrived back home. The hours of meticulous writing, with intense focus and passion, helped restore my purpose. Determination and excitement returned as I thought about the committee's expectations.

Dr. Bill Stanley, a great friend and also a member of the Clinical Examination Committee, knew how vital this meeting was to me. And he was committed to my personal well-being.

Bill anticipated an uphill battle just getting to the meeting. Anita and I considered flying, but Bill convinced us to let him drive. Due to the events of 9/11, he thought flying would be too risky. The heightened awareness of terrorism meant potential anxiety about flying and more time wading through security. Plus, it would have been very tiring for me. And there was always the possibility of my wheelchair getting lost. It made more sense to drive, and Bill gladly made the sacrifice for us.

Weeks in advance, Anita called the hotel in Chicago and asked about a room with a roll-in shower. She was assured there would be no problem. But when we arrived at check-in, we discovered there was no such thing!

Fortunately, we had brought a portable shower chair, which was adaptable to bathtubs. But it was still in the original shipping box and needed to be assembled.

"We can figure this out," Bill calmly assured me.

With a little difficulty and a few complications, Bill and Anita assembled it and adapted it to the bathtub. It wasn't the most pleasant way to shower, but it did accommodate my need.

After a decent night's sleep, I eagerly shaved, combed my hair, got dressed, and put on my favorite cufflinks. I was ready for this challenge! My loyal office staff had helped me design a polished PowerPoint presentation. The combined effort infused me with confidence. But I still had a twinge of anxiety.

This would be the first time an important group of colleagues would see me in a wheelchair, and I was a bit nervous about their first impressions of me.

During the elevator ride to the meeting room area, I offered up a quick, silent prayer. *Heavenly Father, I need an extra shot of confidence right now. Please give it to me, Lord. Thank you. Amen.*

My adrenaline was sky-high as I rolled down the hallway toward the conference room, filled with all thirty board members and examiners.

As I entered, the room became silent. I couldn't help but wonder what they were all thinking and feeling.

When the time came for me to begin my presentation, I started by giving a heartfelt acknowledgment of the special hospital visits by Drs. Ayres, Librizzi, and Bonanno. I wanted everyone to know how important their time and encouragement were to me.

I paused to regain composure and dry my eyes. Before I could speak again, everyone in the room stood, in unison, and applauded vigorously. I couldn't believe it. I certainly hadn't expected that to happen.

Encourage one another and build each other up, just as in fact you are doing. 1 Thessalonians 5:11

My presentation went off without a glitch. When it ended, I realized I had accomplished an important task. I prayed it would be a solid step toward regaining my full responsibility and privileges in the osteopathic OB/GYN community.

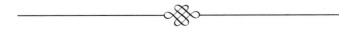

Brad and Raquel showed up to celebrate my success. They insisted on going to the historic Drake Hotel in downtown Chicago for lunch. The hotel had a special dining room we'd enjoyed on previous visits. I was exhausted but too touched to say no to their request.

The taxi ride to the restaurant was a fiasco. Apparently, Chicago cabbies weren't used to wheelchair passengers. Transferring into the vehicle was difficult because the driver pulled right up against the curb, making it hard for Anita to get me out of the wheelchair and into the backseat. We faced the same situation at our destination, as the cabbie again parked right next to the curb.

When we entered the hotel, we were told there was no direct access to the restaurant for people in wheelchairs. Diners had to walk up a full flight of stairs to get into the dining room.

"You've got to be kidding," I exclaimed. "This is important to us. There's got to be a way to get me up there. I don't care how you do it—just make it work!"

The dining room manager granted us permission to use the service elevator through the kitchen. I hated making a scene. But at least we managed to have a memorable dinner.

On our last day in Chicago, all of the examiners and board members, as well as my wife and children, went out to dinner at Nick's Fish Market. We all sat at one long table.

I was caught off guard when several among the group stood to give testimonials about me. Many of them told my children about my professional accomplishments over the years. I wasn't prepared for their effusive praise. My confidence soared. *Thank you, Lord!*

Whoever humbles himself like this child is the greatest in the kingdom of heaven. MATTHEW 18:4

The next day, when we got into the car to return home, I told Anita and Bill I wanted to take off the front of my turtle brace. "And I don't want anyone to argue with me about it!"

They argued anyway.

But I didn't let them stop me. "That thing has been driving me crazy all weekend, and I'm tired of it. Riding in a car without it won't hurt one bit. I'm not going to be moving around, so there won't be a problem," I justified. "It's my decision. Period!"

Anita sighed, shaking her head in disapproval. But she didn't say a word. Neither did Bill.

I reached under my loose pullover sweater and released the Velcro straps on the front piece—by myself—and handed it to Anita in the backseat. It felt really good to not have the hard plastic digging into my neck. The relief it gave me was the same as before my accident after removing my shoes.

I'd already tilted the seat back to be more comfortable. So every time the car turned or stopped, I didn't have to worry about keeping my balance. I was determined not to cause any trouble.

Upon arriving home, I put on the turtle brace before getting out of the car. Wearing it while moving around was still necessary.

An unexpected sense of comfort covered me when we entered the condo. I felt secure and relaxed. It was a consequence of my new sense of confidence. I had accomplished my first professional goal by giving the Chicago presentation.

The long day ended with prayers of gratitude and reflection. Having a new memory echo in my heart was a joy. Feeling successful was awesome.

A good night's sleep was in order. Instead, I immediately started imagining my next adventure.

17

Press On

*Healing is a matter of time,
but it is sometimes also a matter of opportunity.*
HIPPOCRATES

For the first time since coming home from the hospital, my anxiety didn't overwhelm me as I watched Anita drive off to work. I was alone, but felt less lonely. Yet the quest for a successful life wasn't easy.

Dr. Nieshoff told me, "This first year is going to be tough because everything will be new for you." His words helped me confront numerous hurdles and character-building challenges.

In the continued face of adversity, fear, and anxiety, I focused on God and the future. That enabled me to keep my determination intact in spite of the circumstances. This was a critical strategy for moving forward, especially with serious questions to answer and important decisions to make. To succeed, I needed God at the forefront of everything.

I pray also that the eyes of your heart may be enlightened in order that you may know the hope to which he has called you, the riches of his glorious inheritance in the saints, and his incomparably great power for us who believe. That power is like the working of his mighty strength, which he exerted in Christ when he raised him from the dead and seated him at his right hand in the heavenly realms. EPHESIANS 1:18–20

I looked forward to a brighter future. But insecure thoughts persisted.

Can I still be a doctor?

Will I remain the OB/GYN residency program director?

Are my dreams of being an ACOOG leader realistic?

Only time would reveal the answers. Without a doubt, the events to come would either make or break me. I was determined to succeed.

I was enthusiastic about an invitation Pastor Armistead had given me while I was still in the hospital. He had asked me to give my testimony to the congregation on December second, the first Sunday in Advent. My Chicago achievement provided the momentum I needed to start planning what to share. I only had five weeks to prepare.

I had dreamed many times about giving a sermon, but I'd never imagined doing it from a wheelchair. I considered this both a privilege and a responsibility. Sharing my life publicly meant putting my integrity on the line. Being authentic was of utmost importance to me. I asked God for guidance and to keep me faithful and strong as I planned my talk.

The man of integrity walks securely, but he who takes crooked paths will be found out. PROVERBS 10:9

God blessed me with focus as I prepared my testimony. I wanted to praise him and demonstrate his love through my story. My hope was to show people how I trusted the Lord so they could do the same. In order to deepen their faith, I would need to penetrate their hearts.

Music provided a great deal of inspiration as I worked. Listening to certain songs was like praying for me. Every day I listened to CDs of my favorite gospel group, Selah. Their music provided the inspiration I needed.

Selah's album *Press On* won the Gospel Music Association's Dove Award for Inspirational Album of the Year in 2002. My favorite song on that album is "Press On." It was a breakout song for Selah, hitting the music world in the summer of 2001—the same time as my accident.

Press On

When the valley is deep,

When the mountain is steep,

When the body is weary,

When we stumble and fall,

When the choices are hard,

When we're battered and scarred,

When we've spent our resources,

When we've given our all,

In Jesus' name, we press on.

In Jesus' name, we press on.

Dear Lord, with the prize

Clear before our eyes,

We find the strength to press on.

In Jesus' name, we press on.

In Jesus' name, we press on.[3]

During the transition to my new life, I played that song over and over, connecting with the lyrics. That was how I worshipped God during my loneliest times and beyond.

One day in early November, Pastor Armistead stopped by to see me. He asked about the title of my talk so he could include it in the church bulletin. It hadn't occurred to me to come up with a title. But after a thoughtful pause, an idea popped into my head.

"Press On," I said.

His right eyebrow arched. "You mean, like the title of the Selah song?"

"Exactly."

He chuckled. "Jim Smith is going to be in church this Sunday. He's the father of Todd and Nicole, two of the three Selah singers. He's one of the missionaries we support."

"You're kidding me!" No way was this is a coincidence.

Pastor Armistead introduced me to Jim following church on Sunday.

After a few minutes of small talk, I said, "I'm giving my testimony to the congregation on December second. The title is 'Press On.' I chose that theme in part because of the Selah song."

He smiled. "I'm sure it will be a great testimony."

I took a deep breath. "Do you think there's any chance Selah could be here that day?"

He hesitated. "I doubt it. They've been in great demand since 9/11. But I'll tell them about our conversation and how important their song is to you. I'm sure they'll at least write you a letter."

"That would be very nice." I was learning to accept disappointment, so I didn't overreact or attempt to use any of my infamous persuasion tactics.

When I told Anita about my request, she laughed. "You didn't really think they could come, did you?"

I shrugged. "Actually, I have a feeling God's in this. I believe it just might happen!"

A week later, Pastor Armistead called and told me that Selah had said they would come and sing "Press On"!

After that great news I was more eager than ever to continue preparing for my talk and to get my turtle brace off.

Dr. Nieshoff wrote orders for my outpatient rehab to begin in October. But I decided to wait until my turtle brace was removed permanently. Dr. McCormick insisted I wear it for twelve weeks. That meant I'd be wearing it until mid-November.

I counted the days until that nuisance could come off.

When the time of freedom arrived, I awoke with great anticipation. Anita and I followed our usual morning routine. But when she reached for the turtle brace I stopped her. "I'm not wearing that thing anymore."

Anita froze with a wrinkled brow. "What do you mean?"

"I was scheduled to wear this for twelve weeks. Today is November fifteenth—twelve weeks to the day!"

"You have to wait until you see the neurosurgeon next week," she insisted.

"I am not waiting. This thing is going into the trash today, and I never want to see it again."

"I think you're making a big mistake," she argued.

"My decision is final." And that was the end of the discussion.

Carefully, we finished getting me dressed and into my wheelchair. I was wobbly as I sat there for the first time without the brace.

It felt great to finally be free of the cumbersome contraption. But as I rolled from the bedroom to the kitchen, I was unstable. The turtle brace had provided more support than I realized. My core muscles were not used to holding up my body on their own. I had to work hard to sit up and not fall forward. I was weaker than I thought and paid the price of extra pain. But I never once considered putting the turtle brace back on—not even for a second.

Terri, one of the nurses at my OB/GYN office, had a home-health background, working with rehab patients. She expressed a desire to help me in any way she could.

Terri volunteered to drive me to outpatient rehab three times a week. Instead of just dropping me off at my appointments, she stayed and got involved in the rehab exercises.

We used my transfer board, which made it easier for me to get in and out of her compact car. She also helped with dignity issues. More than once, I lost bowel control in Terri's new car. I cringed in embarrassment and humiliation, but Terri simply cleaned up the mess. In an effort to make it up to her, I bought slipcovers to protect her car seats. It was the least I could do!

The outpatient routine was an extension of my former inpatient situation with some added work. Instead of transferring from my wheelchair to a bench at the same level, it was mandatory for me to practice lifting myself four or five inches to a higher bed or chair. Doing this required more upper-body strength, balance, and determination. Additionally, the physical therapist had me go up and down curbs and hills. Terri spotted for me and encouraged me.

I sweated through the strenuous workout. But for me, the standard outpatient regimen was too basic. I progressed more quickly than the average patient and demanded even more.

One day I showed up early to lift weights. I was told weight training wasn't part of my plan. That meant no one could help me. But I worked out anyway.

The exercise routine was aimed at improving balance and practicing transferring. But there was nothing geared toward strengthening the upper body. I decided to find a personal trainer who could help me establish a more thorough exercise program.

Family and close staff members investigated my options. Laurie made several phone calls. Anita asked people at the hospital. Word got around quickly.

Dr. Aaron Tragos, an osteopathic orthopedic surgeon at Riverside, got wind of my situation. He called Skip Bunton, a certified personal trainer known for his success in treating athletes with sports-related injuries. Skip founded and owned Body Specs Inc. Dr. Tragos was confident he would be a good match for me.

Skip's first response sounded negative. "I'm not set up like a physical therapy clinic," he told Dr. Tragos. "My process is too intensive for a spinal-cord-injury patient."

Dr. Tragos persisted, insisting that Skip's techniques would work with me. Skip finally agreed to call me.

"I'm Skip Bunton with Body Specs," he said in a strong voice. "My experience is with athletes recovering from injuries."

"That's what I've heard. But Dr. Tragos strongly recommended you."

"Most spinal-cord-injury patients need extra TLC because of the drastic life changes involved. TLC's not my game."

"Try me."

Our brief conversation led to an appointment for a face-to-face meeting at Body Specs, though I didn't hold out much hope for a positive collaboration. I doubted this narrow-minded, arrogant guy cared one bit about what I had in mind.

I was wrong!

The first time I rolled into his facility, I stopped abruptly at the door. This was no powerhouse gym. It was a place for real athletes. Men and women were doing strenuous floor exercises, some were boxing, and others were throwing a medicine ball. Timers rang when it was time for individuals to move on to another exercise. Everyone appeared to be in good shape. And no one was overweight.

Skip and I shook hands and exchanged a few verbal courtesies. Then I got right to the point. "Can you really get my core muscles back? Can you prepare me for the demands of a rigorous OB/GYN medical practice?"

"Yes, Dr. Wolf, I can," he said with confidence.

Skip backed up his bold statement by explaining his credentials. "I earned my undergraduate degree in biology from Sienna Heights University in 1983. In 1985 I earned a sports medicine master's degree at Indiana State University, specializing in athletic training and rehabilitation of sports-related injuries. I've published many articles and given numerous lectures on my specialized rehab and intensive training techniques. In 2004 and 2005, *Men's Journal* named me one of the top one hundred trainers in the country."

I was impressed.

"My approach to training and rehab has proven highly beneficial for helping injured athletes get back into the game quickly."

Skip's passion, innovative methods, and love of teaching mesmerized me. "That's what I want—to get back into the game as soon as possible."

I candidly explained to Skip my determination to achieve specific goals. "Being in a wheelchair is not going to hinder me. I'm not about to sit back and languish in depression. You won't have to motivate me."

"You and I are more alike than I thought," said Skip. "We're both focused, goal oriented, and not easily distracted from getting what we want. It sounds like we both see adversity as a challenge. And we both believe in hard work!"

That was all I needed to hear. I was convinced this man could get me to the next level of strength and endurance for re-entering the demands of my medical practice.

Skip put me on his schedule for one hour, three days a week. We agreed to start the first week in December.

The timing was perfect. It allowed me to focus completely on finalizing my testimony before beginning another new routine.

On Advent Sunday, I stood on the stage, facing the congregation with great anticipation. Selah led the program with *It Is Well with My Soul.*

It Is Well with My Soul

When peace, like a river, attendeth my way,

When sorrows like sea billows roll;

Whatever my lot, Thou has taught me to say,

It is well, it is well with my soul.

Refrain:

It is well, with my soul,

It is well, it is well, with my soul.

My sin—oh, the bliss of this glorious thought!—

My sin, not in part but the whole,

Is nailed to the cross, and I bear it no more.

Praise the Lord, praise the Lord, O my soul!

And Lord, haste the day when my faith shall be sight,

The clouds be rolled back as a scroll;

The trump shall resound, and the Lord shall descend.

Even so, it is well with my soul.[4]

To my amazement, Todd looked at me as they sang, tears rolling down his cheeks.

After being lifted up by this beautiful song and the faith-filled voices of Nicole Sponberg, Todd Smith, and Alan Hall, I felt embraced by God's love and totally free to begin my talk. Here are some excerpts from it:

This is a special day in the Christian community. It marks the first Sunday in Advent. Advent is the time to prepare ourselves for the coming of Jesus Christ. Jesus was born in Bethlehem in a manger with the common animals of the day. It is not the way you and I would have told the story, but it was God's way of letting us know about something special.

Jesus never walked very far from home. He didn't have a college education, and he never wore a crown of jewels. In fact, in the end, he had a crown of thorns. This one man changed the world of that day and continues to change the world today for you and me.

His message was simple yet profound. He said to all those who would listen, "Come, follow me. If you say yes, I will give you the courage to press on. I will carry you when you can't walk. I will give you gifts to glorify my name. And if that is not enough, I will give you eternal life."

Isn't it amazing how the people of that day and the people of this day, and probably some people in this church, have rejected his call? Some people say, "Why would Jesus want me? I'm nobody. I have no special gifts."

They don't understand the message. God made us all special. No two people have the same fingerprints, not even identical twins. God has given all of us unique gifts to glorify his name.

Following this introduction, I talked about how Jesus had been in my heart since the early days of my life. (To hear my full "Press On" testimony, please visit www.TheGiftIsYou.org.)

The Lord's awesome presence filled the church with joy, hope, and promise that day. I wondered what God had up his sleeve with this unexpected gift of speaking influence.

> **If anyone is in Christ, he is a new creation; the old has gone, the new has come!** 2 CORINTHIANS 5:17

Almost three months after coming home to a new life, in spite of all the frustrations and disappointments, I now had hope and a sense of confidence about my future.

I felt good about turning my loss into something that could benefit others, just as the actions of others had benefited me.

Of course, the path would not be easy. I still had lessons to learn. But God evidently had something planned for my future, with opportunities specifically orchestrated by him. I knew, beyond a doubt, that I would press on.

> **Brothers, I do not consider myself yet to have taken hold of it. But one thing I do: Forgetting what is behind and straining toward what is ahead, I press on toward the goal to win the prize for which God has called me heavenward in Christ Jesus.** PHILIPPIANS 3:13–14

18

Milestones

One can never consent to creep when one has an impulse to soar.
HELEN KELLER

On the first day of my exercise program at Body Specs, Skip took me into a private assessment room, transferred me onto the exam table, and manually pumped my legs. Ten minutes on one side and ten minutes on the other side. "The legs are sixty-five percent of the body's total weight. Moving them like this will help keep your hips and knees flexible."

My dead weight was a hefty workout for him. But I could do nothing to help.

After he put me back in my chair, we went to the main gym area. He made me wear a twenty-pound weighted vest, secured with Velcro straps, before beginning a series of exercises coordinated specifically for me. "This will provide stability and added resistance to your core muscles while you work," he explained.

Skip handed me a weighted jump rope to use for the first exercise. My job was to lift the rope over my head and swing it forward to the floor as if I were going to jump rope and then reverse the move.

My heart pounded, and my face dripped with sweat. But I continued the exercise until the timer sounded. That ding was music to my ears!

Next I rolled over to a five-foot-tall heavy bag, suspended from the ceiling, the bottom two feet from the floor. Skip gave me boxing gloves to put on and then demonstrated how to punch the bag for maximum results.

"Okay, Dr. Wolf. Give it all you've got!"

I punched that thing until I was breathless. By the time I finished the exercise, my arm and shoulder muscles ached, my heart was beating like a drum, and my shirt was wringing wet.

The last set of exercises was done with a medicine ball. I faced the wall and threw the ball, allowing it to bounce before catching it again. After twenty reps, I

Developing core muscles and cardiovascular strength using a heavy bag

turned sideways and did twenty more, again allowing the ball to bounce before catching it.

We then moved on to a game of catch. Skip tossed the medicine ball to me, and I returned it. Then he moved back a few feet and we did it again. When Skip got to the opposite side of the room from me, he threw the ball hard to reach me. When I caught it, the ball's momentum knocked me over. I fell back, hitting the floor with a thud.

Skip leaped toward me. "You all right?" he asked as he flipped me upright.

"I'm okay." Though adrenaline raced through me at the shock, I wasn't hurt.

"I think that's enough for your first day." Skip walked beside me on the way to the lobby. "Sure you want to come back for more torture?"

"I'm game if you are." I winked. "I think this was as much torture for you as it was for me."

When I returned to the gym, I discovered Skip had drilled two holes into the floor and installed an eyehook in each one. He put a strap around the lower part of my chair and ratcheted it down to lock me in place so I wouldn't flip.

"Great strategy!" I told him.

"I thought so."

Skip's innovative techniques were nothing like RIM's routine. The work was hard, but I loved it. Improvements in my posture, reflexes, and upper-body strength made a huge difference in my balance and in my ability to transfer more efficiently. And I became less breathless as I exercised, which was an indication of improved cardio endurance. Beyond all these benefits, the strengthening routine made an immeasurable contribution to my confidence and dignity.

Fighting back using a medicine ball during my first days at Body Specs

Terri insisted on driving me to Body Specs, even though she admitted she was not a big fan of exercise. Naturally, I encouraged her to participate.

One day, as Terri and I were playing catch with the medicine ball, I turned my head in response to a question Skip asked. At the same second, Terri released the ten-pound ball.

I heard it bounce, but couldn't turn around fast enough to prevent it from hitting my face. It knocked off my glasses, and my nose started spurting blood.

Terri rushed to my side. "We've got to get you to a hospital!"

"No, no, I'm okay." I wiped blood from my upper lip. "Just grab me some cotton."

She scurried off and came back with a couple of cotton balls, which I inserted into my nostrils to stop the bleeding.

Skip brought me back my glasses, which were badly bent.

"Oh, Dr. Wolf, I am so sorry," Terri moaned.

Recognizing the opportunity for a teachable moment, I said, "You know, when something unexpected happens, you don't quit. You improvise, adapt, and keep going."

She nodded. "I'll remember that."

I hoped I'd planted a seed of encouragement in her.

Thanks to Terri's tender heart and helpful hands and Skip's knowledge, techniques, and work ethic, I made great strides the first year. Going to Body Specs became part of my weekly routine. It was a great accomplishment and milestone on the path of my new life. But the results went much deeper than my body conditioning. Skip and I became mentors for each other.

> **I know that there is nothing better for men than to be happy and do good while they live. That everyone may eat and drink, and find satisfaction in all his toil—this is the gift of God.** ECCLESIASTES 3:12–13

Despite adapting to new situations and a rigorous personal training commitment, I was still left with too many hours at home by myself. I felt lonely. Questions and insecurity continued to flood my mind. But through prayer and meditation, I started appreciating the quiet alone time—something that had been nonexistent in my past, over-scheduled life.

Solitude gave me time to think deeply about my future as I contemplated one of the most critical decisions of my life: *Do I continue doing deliveries and surgeries?*

I knew many of my patients would allow me to perform these procedures on them. And several staff members had promised to work alongside me during deliveries and surgeries. The possibility certainly appealed to me. I wanted desperately to maintain my former identity.

Although patients and staff had enough confidence in me, I questioned myself.

Will I have the same precision as before when a delicate surgery is needed?

Will I have the stamina to handle a three-hour surgery?

Can I get to the hospital fast enough when a delivery is imminent?

But giving up deliveries and surgeries could mean losing the respect of my residents.

Will I still be credible as an OB/GYN program director?

Will I have something to offer even though I won't be walking the delivery and surgery halls with my residents anymore?

Will I be able to relate to them in the special way I've always done?

A lot was at stake here.

My decision would be permanent, leaving no alternative to turn back. It was a choice I'd have to live with for the rest of my life. Uncertainty provoked great anxiety.

I needed someone to help me make the decision. But I didn't know any other paraplegic OB/GYN surgeons!

Once again, the powerful privilege of prayer brought me through. I knew I was put on earth to please God and live like Jesus. So I prayed.

Show me your way, Lord. I cannot do this without you. Help me accept that you are in control. I want to serve you and be happy with what you give me. I am humble in your presence. I'm afraid, but I trust you. Thank you for understanding my weaknesses. Please help me, Father, to put my will aside. I am completely turning my life over to you. I am waiting and listening for your answer. I love you. Amen.

I prayed the same thing over and over. This required a leap of faith and tremendous humility.

After many days of seeking God's heart, the answer became clear. Continuing as before would be a gamble for my patients. The last thing I wanted to do was jeopardize their health.

The risks seemed to outweigh the rewards of continuing.

When I calmly told people I'd decided to no longer do deliveries and surgeries, they were surprised. But after releasing my burden to God and giving it over to him, I felt free. His supernatural power gave me confidence to be bold in my quest for a future led by him.

> **If any of you lacks wisdom, he should ask God, who gives generously to all without finding fault, and it will be given to him. But when he asks, he must believe and not doubt, because he who doubts is like a wave of the sea, blown and tossed by the wind. That man should not think he will receive anything from the Lord; he is a double-minded man, unstable in all he does.** JAMES 1:5–8

I trusted God to bring new blessings into my life. But I also accepted that with new joys, there would be fresh and unexpected hurdles to overcome.

19

Defining Moments

*Things turn out best for those who
make the best out of how things turn out.*
JOHN WOODEN

The new year arrived with traditional events. One annual ritual remained intact thanks to a special group of friends: my football buddies. We rarely missed the New Year's Day games on TV at Chuck Rossi's house.

Frank drove me to Chuck's place. Being a big, strong guy, it was easy for him to help transfer me in and out of the car. After parking, he insisted on taking me down to Chuck's basement recreation room, where Chuck's dad and sons were gathered, along with my other good friend, Bob Sauter.

Frank confidently grabbed the handles of my wheelchair, tilted it back, and slowly lowered me down the first of fourteen steps.

On about the third stair, Frank's legs gave out. The wheelchair slipped out of his hands and bounced all the way to the bottom. Since I wasn't strapped in, I slid out and landed on my back.

"Are you all right?" Frank yelled.

"Are you kidding?" I chuckled. "I can't feel a thing. Are you okay?"

Everyone bolted toward me. Before I could catch my breath, I was back in my chair.

Frank stared at me, his face ashen. "What if—"

I cut him off before he could say another word. "We don't need to talk about the what-ifs because nothing bad happened."

The rest of the day I focused on the football games and, more important, the gift of friendship. I was grateful to know that some things would always remain the same.

Although the incident wasn't funny at the time, it gave my friends and me something to joke about later. Whenever we tell this story, Frank always says, "Hey, you told me to drop you off at Chuck's, and that's exactly what I did!"

A friend loves at all times, and a brother is born for adversity.
PROVERBS 17:17

January 2002 started with a bang (pun intended). But after enjoying the camaraderie of good friends, I had to focus on preparation for January 14, the date I'd set for my return to work.

I was unsure of my ability to continue as a physician. But I didn't want to give up my dreams. Ultimately, there was just one question I needed to answer: was I willing to put my trust in God?

Two important strategies provided a solid foundation for moving forward: daily prayer conversations with God and nightly reflection on his Word, with Anita reading to me from the Bible. The essential ingredient for success was to pay attention to him, not to myself.

Have I not commanded you? Be strong and courageous. Do not be terrified; do not be discouraged, for the Lord your God will be with you wherever you go. JOSHUA 1:9

I didn't know how my life was going to work out, but I did know God had great things in store for me.

With this perspective I began addressing the tasks necessary to meet my January 14 goal.

First, I needed my own wheelchair. I'd been renting one, and a physical therapist from RIM had ordered a new one for me from a medical equipment company, but for some reason the order got lost. I called and told them they'd better get me a wheelchair fast or there was going to be a big problem.

When it finally arrived, I smiled at it. This wheelchair wasn't my enemy. *You and I are going to be companions for a long time, my friend.* It was a defining moment.

I also needed to get an exam table that would raise patients to my height in the wheelchair. Several staff members took turns driving me around town to medical offices to see the different types available. I didn't think it was going to be a problem. But every exam table had a footplate at the end to make it easier for patients to get onto the table. The footplates extended out approximately twelve inches. That would make it impossible for me to get close enough to examine patients.

No problem. I'll just have a customized table made.

But due to liability issues, no manufacturer would take the risk.

My hope of continuing as an OB/GYN physician began to crumble.

One week before I was scheduled to begin seeing patients, Laurie phoned me. "Dr. Wolf, a salesman came in here today with a catalog of exam tables without footplates."

"Really?" I was skeptical, but wondered if there might be a thread of hope here. "Tell him to bring one to the office for me to evaluate."

As I waited for the table to arrive, I prepared myself for disappointment. If this didn't work, it was going to be a big blow for me.

I prayed a lot.

When the exam table arrived, it was set up in the largest exam room—the only one big enough for me to move around in to examine patients.

I took a deep breath before entering the room. Then I rolled in—and right up to the end of the table.

"I can do exams!" I whimpered, then started crying.

Everyone around me cried too.

It is by grace you have been saved, through faith—and this not from yourselves, it is the gift of God—not by works, so that no one can boast. For we are God's workmanship, created in Christ Jesus to do good works, which God prepared in advance for us to do. EPHESIANS 2:8–10

THE GIFT IS YOU

The remaining tasks fell easily into place. My office desk was raised and my work station lowered. Since the restrooms were already handicap-accessible for patients, no changes were needed there.

But a third potential obstacle presented itself that I hadn't considered before. *How am I going to enter the building?* The employee entrance at the side of the building had a concrete step—no ramp.

My family and staff suggested I enter through the automatic doors at the public entrance.

That wasn't the answer I wanted to hear. "Doctors don't come through the patient waiting area to get to their offices!"

My staff suggested building a side-entrance ramp. But I didn't like the idea of being different from everyone else. "The building stays as is," I insisted.

On January 14, Anita drove me to the side door. One of the office employees met me there and rolled my wheelchair up the step and into the building. That arrangement suited my ego just fine!

Those who walk in pride he is able to humble. DANIEL 4:37

To my delight, I had eight patients scheduled on my first day back. But insecurity crept in.

Will my patients be shocked when they see me?

Will they think I look different?

Will they pity me?

Will they be overly sympathetic?

I knew I was the same person, but their perception of how I'd do as their doctor was critical. I didn't want anyone to feel sorry for me or define me by my wheelchair.

Entering the exam room for the first time since my accident six months before felt like a big risk. I hesitated before rolling in to see my first patient. Doubts continued to whirl in my head.

With sweaty palms and heart pounding, I told myself, *Just do it!*

Gathering all my courage, I opened the door.

The exam room immediately felt like home. I said hello, and my patient and I exchanged friendly pleasantries. I got caught up on the

- 126 -

latest happenings in her life. Then, just as thousands of times before, I proceeded with the exam.

Everything went flawlessly. It was another defining moment.

The first week ended on a high note on January 20, when my second interview with *The News-Herald* was published. The headline read, "Doctor on the Mend: Faith Defines Recovery for David Wolf."

The story covered my accident, recovery, exercising, seeing patients again, and an important message: "Believe in God no matter what happens in your life." (See Appendix 5 for full text of this article.)

I appreciated the newspaper staff for investing time, effective writing, talented photography, and prime space in the Sunday paper for a non-celebrity.

After seeing my letter and two interviews published in the paper, friends joked, "Hey, Dr. Wolf, what are we going to read about you next?"

The attention I got was a boost. But I was troubled with constant

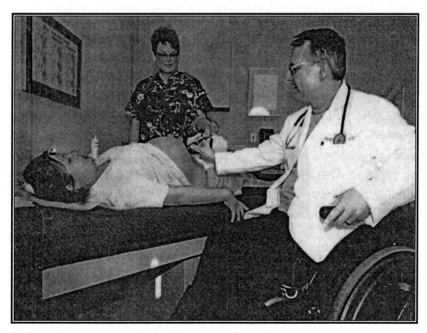

Back to work examining a patient, while my nurse, Terri Little Loeckner, assists

insecurity, even though the public and my patients seemed to accept me back into the medical community.

I needed to make sure they weren't coming to see me just to make me feel good. So I put together an evaluation form with four questions and a comment section. Terri gave a copy of the form to each patient after the exam was completed, suggesting they could take it home and mail it anonymously if they wished. Amazingly, everyone I examined wanted to complete and sign it on the spot!

I looked at each questionnaire before going on to the next appointment. My need for reinforcement was great. Their responses proved what I had hoped to be true: I was okay, and my practice would be okay.

One comment especially delighted me: "Dr. Wolf, it's going to take more than a wheelchair to get you out of this!"

We continued the questionnaire for about two months. One day Terri said, "I don't think we need this anymore. Your patients are all happy. Can we stop now?"

I enjoyed the "pats on the back"—a little too much. I agreed that we could stop the process.

Before my accident, God had given me the privilege of delivering more than eleven thousand babies and performing approximately twenty surgeries a week. I couldn't maintain that strenuous schedule now. It was essential for me to exercise three times a week so I'd have enough strength, energy, and endurance to provide excellent patient care. I came to the conclusion that to do my best I could only schedule appointments two days a week.

That was one tough decision. I'd always felt it was a sign of defeat to work less than eighteen-hour days, six days a week.

My father had instilled in me a strong work ethic. He delivered milk for Med-O-Bloom Dairy most of his life, and he consistently demonstrated the qualities of responsibility, working hard, and doing his best.

When I was in sixth grade, Dad insisted that I help on his milk truck. My alarm went off at three o'clock every Saturday morning from age eleven through my senior year in high school.

At first it was fun waking up before dawn to be with my father. I was proud to be his partner and I felt important carrying cases of milk into the stores.

The novelty wore off as I got a little older. Friday night was date night, and getting up at three on Saturday wasn't fun anymore. But according to my dad, delivering milk was still my priority.

"You made a commitment, Dave," he'd remind me. "Life isn't always easy. But no complaints. Now, let's go!"

He expected me to do my best. Always. No matter what.

Yet I'm certain he never intended for me to become a workaholic.

The only relief came in God's answers to my prayers. He helped me keep things in perspective. I had no other means of controlling my feelings of diminished worth.

> **You were taught, with regard to your former way of life, to put off your old self, which is being corrupted by its deceitful desires; to be made new in the attitude of your minds.** Ephesians 4:22–23

Anita and I were still undecided about the kind of van to purchase. And I needed to complete a special training program before I could get a handicapped driver's license. So on the two days a week I saw patients, she dropped me off at nine o'clock in the morning on her way to work, then picked me up at six on her way home.

Even after we bought a van and I got my license, Anita continued driving me to the office. It made sense to carpool, and it was more comfortable for me.

Over time, I started working longer hours. Six o'clock turned into seven, eight, nine, and sometimes later.

Anita's bedtime was about nine o'clock, but she was willing to accommodate my progressively long hours—temporarily.

After about three months of this schedule, Terri called my wife on a Thursday night to tell her we were running late . . . again.

Anita showed up at eleven and I still wasn't finished seeing patients.

She sat in my private office and waited another hour.

When we finally got in the car, she said calmly, "David, we had a deal. You promised you weren't going to be a workaholic anymore. I thought we were going to spend more time together. I thought we would at least be having dinner together." Not once did she raise her voice.

"But taking care of women's health is my passion, and many of my patients need evening appointments. I can't just turn them away."

"I understand that patient care is your priority, David. But if you intend to keep working until midnight, I'm not driving you to the office anymore."

It wasn't a threat. She wasn't forcing me to stop. She just wasn't going to support this lifestyle.

"Okay," I said.

On Monday morning I got in the van, drove myself to the office, and continued to work until midnight.

It was another defining moment in my life.

20

Deciding Factor

Circumstances do not make you what you are.
They reveal what you are.

John Maxwell

Potential barriers to success continued throughout the first year and beyond.

A twinge of sadness tore at my heart every time I heard an intercom message for one of my partners to go to the hospital to deliver a baby. The sound was a reminder that a portion of what I loved was gone forever. I enjoyed the adrenaline rush I used to get as I raced down the alley behind the office to the hospital whenever a delivery was imminent. I couldn't wait to take part in bringing new life into the world.

As time went on, I learned to accept my new lifestyle. But some situations would have happened regardless of my accident.

In late January, during a standard monthly Medical Staff Executive Committee meeting, an announcement was made that Riverside Osteopathic Hospital was in the process of being purchased by the Henry Ford Health System and would soon be closing. Rumors had been spreading for months, but most of us affiliated with the hospital believed this day would never come.

We were given the option to move to Henry Ford Wyandotte Hospital. HFWH had twenty-five OB/GYNs, but the hospital did not have a residency program. It didn't even have interns. And only two of my fellow faculty members, Dr. Al-Jerdi and Dr. Goyert, were seriously considering the move.

I met with Nancy Schlichting, executive vice president and CEO for Henry Ford Health System, to ask if we could continue our program at the new hospital. "I'm responsible for six OB/GYN residents at Riverside. There's no way I'm giving up my commitment to them," I said passionately.

"I appreciate your loyalty, Dr. Wolf. But how do you see yourself handling this situation?"

"I would serve as the program director. And I'd recruit physicians from your hospital to serve as faculty."

"That's ambitious."

"Since I'm not doing deliveries and surgeries anymore and have reduced my practice schedule, I have time to focus on added administrative functions. I'm perfect for the job."

My convincing speech sold Nancy on my idea, and she honored my request. After meeting with the merged group of physicians, she sent a memo on March 22, 2002, stating the hospital's obligation to osteopathic medical education. The memo assured financial and leadership support as well as faculty accreditation support.

In the midst of this transition, I was still plagued with personal hurdles.

One of the biggest challenges was air travel. I knew flying would be necessary for staying closely involved with the American College of Osteopathic Obstetricians and Gynecologists. And I was determined to attend the upcoming ACOOG annual spring convention on Marco Island, Florida. It was the first time I'd be flying as a handicapped passenger. I felt anxious, but I figured the airlines were experts and would know what to do.

Based on my casual observations on previous trips, I expected people in wheelchairs to board before the rest of the passengers. But I was seated last.

The gate agent told me I had to give up my wheelchair and be transferred to an aisle chair before boarding. Worry over the possibility of losing my wheelchair quickly snowballed into anxiety. When the lack of an aisle chair caused a boarding delay, Anita and I had to wait at the end of the Jetway until one became available.

I recalled all the times I'd been on planes, waiting for my flight to take off. I'd grown irritated far more times than I cared to remember. I'd seen people in wheelchairs getting on and off planes, but I never paid much attention to their situation. Now that I was the person in the wheelchair, I was seeing things from a whole new perspective.

The aisle chair finally arrived. It had four wheels, a high back, and a seat that was only about twelve inches wide. A flight attendant helped Anita transfer me to the narrow chair, then fastened the two broad shoulder straps and one lap strap. I should have felt secure. Instead I felt confined and embarrassed.

Anita prepared my wheelchair to be stored with the checked luggage. She put the handle grips and side plates in my backpack. We didn't want to chance losing them. She kept the cushion, knowing that sitting on it would minimize the risk of my getting pressure sores.

Finally, the attendant pushed me down the aisle in the uncomfortable chair. Anita followed, struggling with my loaded backpack, wheelchair seat cushion, and our carry-on luggage—no easy feat. And there was nothing discreet about it.

I felt the stares of my fellow passengers. I imagined them wondering, *Who is this guy? What's his story?* I felt pitied and humiliated.

When we arrived at our row, Anita put the cushion on my assigned seat, then stowed our belongings in the overhead compartment, which was already nearly full. Then she and the attendant lifted me onto the seat. I felt useless.

Once I was situated, I saw the captain and two other flight attendants standing just outside the cockpit, watching. It wasn't their job to help. They didn't know me. And for all I knew, they didn't care. But they couldn't proceed with the flight until I was settled.

What a tiring ordeal for Anita and an awkward situation for me. By the time we took off, both of us were physically and emotionally exhausted.

As the plane finally ascended, I realized gaining control of my emotions was critical if I wanted success in getting to important ACOOG events. After all, airline regulations were not going to change. I needed to learn how to be calm and conserve my energy if I wanted to participate fully and be recognized as a contributor to the college.

When the plane leveled off, I turned to prayer. *Lord, please give me the strength and courage needed to unclutter my mind from negative thoughts and emotions. Help me accept the restrictions and inconveniences I'll face as a wheelchair-bound traveler. Thank you for helping me. Amen.*

Thank God he helped me overcome my extreme emotions in a situation that was out of my control.

> **O Lord, hear my prayer, listen to my cry for mercy; in your faithfulness and righteousness come to my relief.**
> PSALM 143:1

Anita and I continued to travel by air. It gradually became easier. We started doing our best to prepare for the inevitable inconveniences and got less upset with every flight we took. Embarrassing thoughts disappeared. God's power to transform is amazing!

Eventually, embracing adversity became embedded in my character. It was a deciding factor that would affect a future invisible to me yet always visible to God. Prayer kept me connected with his power and helped me stay focused on his perspective.

> **You will surely forget your trouble, recalling it only as waters gone by.** JOB 11:16

21

A Grateful Servant

To know even one life has breathed easier
because you have lived. This is to have succeeded.

RALPH WALDO EMERSON

God has put a great love in my heart for people. Perhaps it's the reason he keeps surprising me with unexpected opportunities to help others. His name is not always mentioned during a situation, but his presence—without a doubt—is there. Sunday, June 9, 2002, was one of those times.

Frank's sons had season tickets to the Detroit Tigers baseball game at Comerica Park, Detroit's new Major League Baseball stadium. Frank asked me to accompany him to the game. It's something we'd done many times in the past. Our seats were on the third-base side of the field, directly above the Tigers dugout.

It was a perfect day for baseball—except for the summer heat. We were facing the sun, and there wasn't much of a breeze.

Frank noticed I was getting pretty hot. He found one of his pals, a familiar usher, and asked if we could move up under the covered area. The seats weren't as good, but they were in the shade, where it felt a little cooler.

Once we were situated, Frank's eyes returned to home plate. He's a serious baseball fan! Mine, on the other hand, glanced around, as usual, taking in all the sights and sounds of Major League Baseball.

When I noticed a ruckus several rows below, my radar zeroed in.

A woman stood up, screaming and shaking her toddler. "My baby! My baby!"

The mother was slapping the child on her back. The little girl was choking.

I grabbed Frank. "See the couple down there with the child? She's in trouble. Go get her, *now!*"

Frank jumped up without hesitation or questioning. He leapt over me, ran to the end of the aisle, and jumped down several rows of steps. Approaching the mother with arms outstretched, he commanded, "Ma'am, give me your child. I'm with a doctor who can help."

In a split second, she released the toddler to Frank. He raced back, shaking like a leaf, and handed her to me.

I set the toddler on my lap, her back to my chest, and began the Heimlich maneuver. She kept choking. I did it a second time.

"Emergency staff is on the way," shouted an usher.

EMTs could provide me with a sixteen-gauge needle to puncture the child's throat if she didn't respond to the Heimlich. I was prepared for this extreme measure if necessary.

People in the nearby stands started hollering.

"Turn her upside down!"

"Blow in her face!"

"Hit her on the back!"

"That's not going to work!"

In spite of the tension in the crowd, I stayed focused. I had to move fast. The child had five minutes to live without breathing—at the most.

On the third compression, the toddler spit out a chunk of hot dog. As small as it was, it could have ended her life in a matter of seconds.

She started crying for Mommy. Sweet music to our ears!

Stadium officials and the emergency team arrived at our row, along with the shaken parents. The mother scooped up the little girl and held her close.

"We need to examine your child at the stadium emergency station," said one of the medical workers. He gently started moving the family toward an exit.

I breathed a sigh of relief, glad that I'd been in the right place at the right time, but also happy to turn the situation over to capable hands.

A few moments later, the father came back to get his wife's purse. He told me his little girl checked out fine and they were going home.

"No!" I shook my head. "Take her to Children's Hospital and have them look her over thoroughly."

"That's what I wanted to do, but the stadium medical team told me there was no need."

"You don't want to take any chances. Food might have gotten into her lungs or may still be lodged in her trachea. The hospital emergency team can take a chest X-ray and check her oxygen level to make sure she's breathing properly."

He agreed to follow my advice.

As he left, I realized that I never got their names. But that didn't matter. The important thing was, a life was saved.

By now the crowd was back in the game, cheering and "coaching" the team. Hot dog, popcorn, and drink venders continued selling their goods as money exchanged hands. Everyone was enjoying the game. But I was reflecting on what had just happened.

What if Frank hadn't invited me to this game in the first place? What if I'd turned down his invitation? If the sun hadn't been so blazing hot, we wouldn't have considered giving up our great seats. If the stadium had been sold out, we wouldn't have been able to switch. If the seats we moved to hadn't been available, I might not have seen this woman and child. If we hadn't been where we were at the moment the little girl began choking, or if Frank hadn't responded immediately to my request to bring her to me, I wouldn't have been able to save her life.

But I was there. And I did.

This wasn't a random event. God worked out all the details so I would be in the right place at the right time. I was a blessed spectator of divine intervention.

There are different kinds of gifts, but the same Spirit. There are different kinds of service, but the same Lord. There are different kinds of working, but the same God works all of them in all men. 1 CORINTHIANS 12:4–6

As the game went on, I silently whispered a prayer of thanksgiving and praise.

Thank you, Father, for allowing me to be your servant today in saving a child's life. Lord, I pray that resistant and skeptical hearts will be open to your power as a result of this beautiful act of grace. I love you and give you all the praise. In Jesus' name I pray. Amen.

After praying, a sense of peace came over me. Once again, God reassured me of my usefulness. I could still make a difference in people's lives. And for that, I was grateful.

22

New Challenges, New Benefits

There isn't a person anywhere who isn't
capable of doing more than he thinks he can.
HENRY FORD

The year 2002 continued to be one of progress for my medical practice and program director responsibilities. My accident had not separated me from relationships with my patients and residents. I was satisfied with my accomplishments and felt pride in my original group of transferring residents. Signing their diplomas was a great honor. What joy and relief I experienced in relying on God's plan and direction in my life!

Dr. Paul Krueger, my friend who had tried to give me his ACOOG presidential ring when I was in the hospital, called in November. Sixteen months had passed since my accident. I was at home in my study doing paperwork when the phone rang.

"Dave, the ACOOG Nominating Committee has recommended you for vice president."

I had dreamed of one day becoming president of the American College of Osteopathic Obstetricians and Gynecologists. For a moment I sat in silence. Tears filled my eyes.

Are they doing this out of pity? Or do they actually believe in me?

The position represented a three-year commitment. After serving as vice president for one year, I would be expected to serve as president-elect for a year, and then as president the third year. I sat back, put my pen down, and cleared my throat. "Do you think I can do this?"

"You've already proven you can. Many members and officers of the organization have witnessed your continued involvement and contributions."

I had been the newsletter editor for twenty years and maintained the position after my accident. And I stayed actively involved as an ACOOG representative to the American Osteopathic Association Editorial Board. Plus, I remained an active executive member of the Residency Evaluation Committee and chaired the Resident Reporter Scholarship Program.

"It's obvious you're still passionate about the college."

That's what I needed to hear. "Thanks, Paul. I'd be honored to serve."

The job would require attending all ACOOG educational conferences and annual conventions. Most of them were held in other states—which meant I'd be traveling by air a lot. Fortunately, I'd already worked through the hassles of flying as a wheelchair-bound passenger.

Normally, when a person is nominated, if the vote is unanimous, the appointment is awarded at the annual spring business meeting. If it's not unanimous, a person from the floor can be nominated and voted in by the general membership. So I wasn't automatically a shoe-in.

As I traveled to the 2003 convention in Scottsdale, Arizona, I wondered if I might be blindsided. But no other nominations were made.

Following standard protocol, the newly appointed president, Dr. Kedrin Van Steenwyk, gave her presidential address, then announced the new board of trustees, the new president-elect, and finally, the new vice president: me!

No time was allotted on the agenda for acceptance speeches. But I was thrilled with my position and looked forward to the three-year term. It was definitely a dream come true!

> **Do not neglect your gift. . . . Be diligent in these matters; give yourself wholly to them, so that everyone may see your progress.** 1 TIMOTHY 4:14–15

As an officer of ACOOG, I was required to attend all of the college's conferences. But several months passed before I attended another out-of-town meeting.

The fall conference was held in Fort Worth, Texas, at the Worthington Hotel. A leadership renewal effort was scheduled on the last two days for ACOOG's board of trustees. I was delighted to learn that the executive director, Dr. Steve Buchanan, had coordinated the event based on the book *The 7 Habits of Highly Effective People.*[5]

The two-day program was thought-provoking. It energized me to make a stronger commitment to meet my personal goals as well as ACOOG's organizational goals.

One of my favorite parts of the program was a video called *And When You Fall.* It told the compelling story of Olympic and world speed-skating champion Dan Jensen. The day he was to compete in the 1988 winter Olympics in Calgary, he learned that his sister had died. He fell twice in front of ninety million people. But he didn't give up. He returned to compete in the 1994 winter Olympics, which he won, breaking world and Olympic records.

That story really spoke to me. I liked its emphasis on the importance of staying focused on your goals—even during tough times.

Watching this video led to some serious reflection for me. We all face adversity, challenges, and failure. What matters is whether we believe in ourselves and refuse to give up. We need to get back up and press on for the gold.

This can only be done by putting God first in our lives. If we've made this commitment, we may fall, but he will always be there to pick us up.

After the program ended, I returned to the conference room, hoping to catch the facilitator, Connie Hurn. I wanted to talk with her privately to thank her for the work she had done and ask a favor. When I arrived, I found her packing up her materials and equipment. She looked up as I rolled into the room.

"Do you have a few minutes to visit before you leave?" I asked.

"Of course," she said with a quick smile. She moved a few chairs away from a cleared-off table so we could sit and talk. We chatted briefly about the program highlights and the days' conversations.

"I really enjoyed the program," I told her.

"It's my favorite one to teach. I try to live by Covey's seven habits. But it takes practice. You just can't give up."

"Commitment and perseverance," I said, nodding. It was fun to speak with someone who shared similar philosophies. "Do you think I could borrow the Dan Jansen video?"

"I need it for a seminar program I'm doing next week," Connie said. "Where do you live?"

"Trenton, Michigan."

She smiled. "I could bring it to you in November when I visit my family in Michigan."

"That would be great! Thank you."

Over the next couple of years, through mutual ACOOG activities, Connie and I developed a friendship. I discovered that she had been praying for a long time to make a difference and was wondering if her efforts as a consultant for ACOOG motivated anyone. As a result of her continued involvement, ACOOG updated its mission and vision statements.

I appreciated Connie's contributions to the college and was impressed by her unwavering work ethic. But most of all, I liked her reliance on God to help her assist others.

My leadership role in the college brought a new sense of responsibility that fueled my adrenaline-driven personality. This job required motivation and high energy on a regular basis—all the more reason to continue my exercise regimen. Excitement filled my days again as I thrived on challenges and dreamed about the future.

Envisioning possibilities has always been a natural part of my inner character. But one person gave me the courage to dream *big:* Christopher Reeve. He was a famous actor, best known for his role as Superman, and he set the stage for people like me.

Paralyzed from a horseback-riding accident in 1995, Reeve had a special bike made to keep his legs moving in anticipation of being able to walk again someday. The bike represented hope.

Relating to him inspired me to ride an electrically stimulated bike too.

Exercising on the bike could help prevent my muscles from atrophying. It was important to maintain my muscle mass in the event that stem-cell surgery became available for my kind of spinal-cord injury. Being able to walk would only become a reality if my muscles could support the bones.

This dream resulted in a new challenge: to find a bike suitable for my needs.

Therapeutic Alliances Inc. in Fairborn, Ohio, seemed to have the one with the greatest potential. Company president James Schorey convinced me to consider the ERGYS 2, his best bike. Anita, Terri, and I traveled to Ohio to check it out.

"The ERGYS 2 uses a special computer to program electrodes attached to the legs, " James explained as he demonstrated how the bike worked. "The electrodes stimulate the leg muscles, enabling them to move the pedals."

That sounded great to me.

Then he forewarned me that some people's muscles don't respond to this type of equipment.

Fearful thoughts immediately struck me.

What if my legs don't react to the electrical current?

What if my muscles can't handle the extra work?

"Give it a try," James encouraged. "Let's see what you can do."

My pride was at stake, but I let him help me on the bike and get me hooked up. He programmed the computer and hit the Start button. To my amazement my paralyzed legs immediately began pedaling!

My elation quickly turned to disappointment when I rode for only thirty seconds.

"You did great for your first time," James said.

His cheerleading provided a much-needed psychological boost. But those results didn't set well with my competitive personality. "I want to ride for thirty minutes, not thirty seconds."

James shook his head. "It'll take at least six months for you to achieve such an aggressive goal."

Only God had the power to help me through this challenge. But I had him on my side.

My decision to purchase the bike was easy due to my competitive nature and desire to accomplish new goals. I needed the bike to help me gain confidence in getting back to the top of the mountain.

I asked Skip if I could store it at Body Specs. He didn't hesitate a bit. His generosity in allowing me to use his space and electricity was a great gift. He agreed to not let anyone else ride it. Having my own bike added a special element to an already fantastic personal training program.

I started riding the bike as soon as it was delivered. But making progress required more than aspiration. It demanded patience, perseverance, and concentrated effort to improve my game.

I wanted the bike and me to become friends. So even when I felt exhausted I kept going. I pushed myself hard. I did my best to improve every time I got on the bike. Thanks to my natural competitive juices, I didn't give in to the frustration of slow progress.

Prayer kept me focused.

God opposes the proud but gives grace to the humble.
JAMES 4:6

Terri continued working out with me. She helped me on and off the bike and provided constant encouragement. Gradually my endurance improved.

After just three months, I hit my goal. A miracle!

With tears running down my sweaty cheeks, I called James. "You're not going to believe this."

"What?"

"I went for thirty minutes today."

"That's fantastic!"

"We need to set a new goal."

"Okay. How about sixty minutes?"

"I'll give it my best."

"I'm sure you can do it."

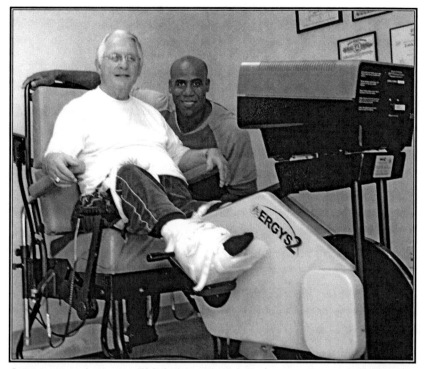

Preparing to work out on my ERGYS 2 bike with the help of my personal trainer, Skip Bunton, Body Specs owner

With the aid of electricity, pedaling exercises reduced the swelling in my legs and ankles, improved my circulation, and minimized problems with bladder infections and bowel movements.

Another benefit was increased muscle mass in my legs, which helped them appear normal. I was still concerned about how I looked and what people might be thinking. This was a dignity and pride issue.

Yet on the bike, I always felt on top of the world. My upper body was in a stationary position, making it easy to look around. I enjoyed observing athletes who were determined to get back in the game. I loved watching them give their best to Skip's demands. And I was encouraged by seeing people who were dedicated and working hard to improve. Everyone at Body Specs had that mind-set. Skip wouldn't have it any other way.

From day one, we were a great team. We all motivated one another and spurred each other on.

The reality of my accident presented two choices: be defeated or fight back. Since real life has no backspace key, fighting back was the only real option for me. I was tenacious and prayed diligently. My faith grew by putting my trust in God. He gave me the physical and spiritual strength to carry on. The entire experience brought me closer to him.

> **I know what it is to be in need, and I know what it is to have plenty. I have learned the secret of being content in any and every situation, whether well fed or hungry, whether living in plenty or in want. I can do everything through him who gives me strength.** PHILIPPIANS 4:12–13

God took my burdens and exchanged them for awesome gifts. His unbelievable power steered the direction of my life. I welcomed moving forward with him and became excited about the possibilities for dreams coming true in unlikely places.

Neither my accident nor my wheelchair handicapped my life.

23

Tragedy Doesn't Just Happen

No God, no peace. Know God, know peace.
ANONYMOUS

Pastor Armistead met me in the Body Specs parking lot as I was getting into my van after a training session. We chatted briefly for a few minutes, then he got right to the point. "The men's ministry group wants you to give another presentation."

I was caught off guard by his invitation. "What do they want to hear from me? My life hasn't changed much since my first talk."

"I'm sure if you pray about it, you'll come up with a very special message."

His response didn't surprise me. He's known as an encourager.

After I agreed to his request, we went our separate ways. While driving home, I started thinking.

It was easy to tell my story when I initiated it. But now I was being asked to give a speech. That was a different situation. There was more pressure, more expectations. Besides, I'd gone back to work and was exercising three days a week. I didn't have a lot of time to plan a presentation. What would I talk about? It would have to be a deep message. It couldn't be just about me.

The more I pondered, the more I realized this was another divine appointment. I was being called to minister to this special group of men, and I could glorify God through my message. This could be an amazing opportunity to demonstrate my personal relationship with Jesus Christ.

I took this responsibility seriously, praying and meditating on it for a long time. My prayers were simple.

Dear Lord, help me bring a message of hope. One that's easy to understand and personally appealing to the men. Please help me express the inner peace in my heart in a way that will be believable and inspiring.

God answered my prayers by revealing to me that it was my job to help these guys climb to the top of their mountains. That was their main need—and the help that I could supply.

When the day arrived for my talk, I was confident and prepared to share God's heart. Frank went with me to the church. The men's group was scheduled to meet in the fellowship hall, where they gathered monthly for breakfast and a special message.

That morning, more than one hundred men showed up. Pastor Armistead had to change the meeting location to accommodate everyone.

As we gathered in the church sanctuary, I was overcome with an even greater sense of responsibility. After all, it isn't often that anyone other than a pastor gives a message from the church altar. My expectations of myself skyrocketed!

I began speaking with a few words of thanks and a prayer for guidance to share the right message—for God.

I followed that prayer with a reflection on my accident. But I quickly moved on to the most important part, which was centered on overcoming adversity through the power of God and a personal relationship with Jesus Christ.

The following is an excerpt from my talk, titled "Tragedy." (Go to www.TheGiftIsYou.org to hear this talk.)

How can someone go from the top of a mountain to the bottom of a valley and still be smiling? I've asked myself that question many times. How could my physical abilities—not to mention my dignity—be taken away, yet my smile continue?

I turned to the Bible for answers and read about a special man named Paul. I also started reading *Paul: A Man of Grace and Grit* by Charles Swindoll.[6] I searched for answers to how Paul could have gone through great tragedy, yet his mission never changed and the twinkle in his eye never went away.

Swindoll said that Paul received his comfort and satisfaction from only one source: Christ Jesus. Paul learned to humbly handle all adversity through the authority of the Lord. And because he gave his trials and fears to him, he was given all the strength he needed to face every situation with confidence.

Life is challenging for all of us. Each person will undergo some form of tragedy while traveling this difficult road. Some may have marriage difficulties, others may have health issues, some may be having problems with their children, and others may be struggling financially.

Sometimes the hardship is long-lived, as it was in Paul's life and as it is in mine. Other times a trial can be short-lived. But to one degree or another, tragedy happens to all of us.

I do not know why God allows such things into our lives. I don't understand why sometimes it lasts for a long period and other times it's a short course. No one really has the answer to that. But I do know that God helps us in these times. He gives us the ability to press on in the trials. He carries us when we can't walk.

I also believe God gives us a special blessing in the midst of our greatest tragedies. Swindoll calls it contentment. The Bible calls it grace. I call it inner peace.

God gives us inner peace. This special blessing is important because we can feel it. We can measure it and we know when we have it. It is perfect for all the struggles we go through.

And the strange thing is, this gift is free. There are no strings attached and no amount of money has to be paid. The only requirement is to believe.

First, you must be a Christian. And you have to give your life to God. If you do, as you go through tragedies, he will give you a blessing and put a twinkle in your eye, just like he did with Paul and me.

Even when guards came to Paul's dirty prison cell in Rome a few minutes before his death, his mission did not change. This is what he said to Timothy before his death:

"I have fought the good fight, I have finished the race, I have kept the faith. Now there is in store for me the crown of righteousness, which the Lord, the righteous Judge, will award to me on that day—and not only to me, but also to all who have longed for his appearing." (2 Timothy 4:7–8)

How can someone go from the top of a mountain to the bottom of a valley and still have a twinkle in his eye? Faith!

The sanctuary was emotionally charged that morning with a spiritual atmosphere greater than I had expected. Those men were clearly there to spend time with God. Most of them had an intensity in their expressions that told me they could personally identify with my message.

God's voice was definitely heard. His presence was evidenced by the group's undivided attention. They were receiving what God wanted them to hear. My hope was that the message would provide a stepping-stone to a better life for all those who were discouraged or experiencing adversity.

At the conclusion of my talk, we returned to the fellowship hall for breakfast. I was pleased with the message, as was Frank.

Jack Westerbeek, a highly recognized member of the church, came up to me and said, "Now I know why you have that twinkle in your eyes."

Jack recognized that I'd received new life in Jesus. He'd heard the message: that we can have joy instead of sorrow, self-esteem instead of despair and depression, and most of all, inner peace instead of a defeatist attitude.

What a gift for me to be a vessel carrying God's hope and encouragement, even if for just one man.

But he wasn't the only person who approached me with comments that made my spirit fly higher than a kite.

"You gave a very powerful talk," said Al Feria, a missionary visiting from Paris. "I think you should write a book including that message."

His words reinforced my own thoughts and gave me the encouragement I needed to turn an idea into a decision.

I knew it would take quite some time to write a book. As I pondered this, Connie Hurn immediately popped into my mind. We had a great friendship and shared similar philosophies. Most important, we both relied on God to help us make a difference in people's lives. I thought she'd be the perfect person to assist me in writing my story. I just hoped she felt the same way.

I prayed right then and there that God would reveal to me when the timing was right to approach her about this project.

My message from that morning was passed on quickly by word of mouth and through CDs of the talk.

I know there are many speakers better than I am, but I had the privilege of sharing the greatest message of all, about God's love and grace. Being a witness to his power became a tremendous blessing for me.

Let us not become weary in doing good, for at the proper time we will reap a harvest if we do not give up.
Galatians 6:9

24

It's Not about Me

We get repeated chances to learn that life is not about us,
that we acquire purpose and satisfaction
by sharing in God's love for others.
Tony Snow

Occasionally the men's ministry group from my church met for breakfast at The Detroiter, a well-known truck stop in southeast Michigan. Originally designed to cater to the traveling public, the restaurant had become a favorite gathering place for diners to relax and enjoy great food in a family setting. Pastor Armistead liked the comfortable surroundings, especially the large meeting room that accommodated up to one hundred people. It was a perfect place for speakers to give talks for the men.

One Sunday morning after church, Pastor Armistead approached me about being a guest speaker there in two weeks. "This will be a casual event," he said nonchalantly, downplaying the invitation.

The timing of his request couldn't have been worse. In a few weeks I'd be inducted as president for ACOOG, and my mind and time had been consumed with preparing a speech for the inauguration ceremony. To top it off, Anita was in the hospital for minor surgery. Being there for her was important to me.

"I'm not sure I have time to do that. I've got a lot on my plate right now."

But Pastor Armistead was persistent. "Don't worry. It's a small group. You only have to talk for about fifteen minutes."

It sounded easy, but I didn't like being put on the spot with little chance to prepare. Then again, maybe I'd have time to write while Anita was having surgery. Hoping Pastor Armistead was right and that this would be a piece of cake, I finally consented.

But as I tried to put thoughts on paper, nothing came to me. Finally, with less than twenty-four hours remaining before the talk, I started to worry.

Maybe there's a way I can get out of this.

I told Anita how I felt.

"Dave, do you really think God is going to let you down on this one?" Her reaction didn't surprise me. She always knows how to put things into perspective. "I'm absolutely certain he wants you to proceed."

I wasn't so sure. Even after going to bed, I suffered silently with anxiety. My only relief was prayer.

Dear Lord, please give me peace to get me through the night. And put the right words in my heart for tomorrow. Thank you.

I hoped the morning would bring to mind something of value to talk about.

I woke up at five o'clock, ready for my usual routine. After drinking a cup of coffee and reading the newspaper, I headed into the bathroom with a pad of paper and a pen. As I sat on the toilet, I meditated, hoping for creative thoughts to jot down. (Seems funny now!)

All of a sudden, words started flowing from my mind. Before I knew it, I had scribbled an outline.

But on the way to the truck stop, I still only had the outline. Doubts plagued me. *Will my message be powerful to anyone?*

Upon arriving at The Detroiter, I rolled into the meeting room, expecting to see only a few people. My eyes about popped out when I saw fifty men sitting at tables arranged in a U-shaped fashion. A portable microphone and speaker system were stationed on the open end of the room. This wasn't going to be a "casual event" after all. These men were expecting another "Dr. Wolf talk." And all I had was an outline.

Ad-libbing wasn't an option. Those guys were depending on me.

I took my seat between Pastor Armistead and John Florek, the men's ministry leader in charge of the event. I strained to be polite by contributing to the small talk as we ate breakfast. But it was hard to relax. *God, are you going to pull me through this time?*

"You ready to roll?" John asked as we finished eating.

Ready as I'll ever be, I thought, but faked an upbeat response. "Let's do it!"

Positioning myself behind the intimidating microphone, I again prayed silently. *God, this is in your hands. Please give me your words.*

As I began to speak, my nerves settled down. God was in control—he was speaking into the microphone through me. My words became his words as I delivered a message titled "Don't Be Destroyed by What Happens to You."

My voice was clear and confident. It reflected a peace that comes only by having Jesus in my life. It was all about him.

Anita was right! The message was amazing, empowered by God's undeniable presence. Through me, he changed people's hearts. How could I have thought for a moment that he might let me down?

Tears filled my eyes during the drive home. After feeling roped into doing something I wasn't prepared to do, I realized once again that God is awesome! He didn't give up on me.

God trusted me more than I trusted myself—or him.

I couldn't wait to tell Anita. Excitedly, I burst into the house. "Anita, you were right! I gave an unbelievable talk this morning. Jesus was in the room! It was so powerful."

She just smiled. She'd known the truth all along.

Do not throw away your confidence; it will be richly rewarded. You need to persevere so that when you have done the will of God, you will receive what he has promised.

HEBREWS 10:35–36

I learned two important lessons that day. First, always be faithful; trust is the key. Second, we don't have to be perfect to do his work; humility is honorable.

The next day, Anita and I attended the eleven o'clock Sunday morning church service, as usual. We sat close to the back of the sanctuary, same as always.

Before beginning his sermon, Pastor Armistead acknowledged my testimony given for the men's ministry group at The Detroiter. Then he expounded on another testimony given Saturday night by Frank Turner, a local celebrity and renowned television broadcaster who had been hooked on drugs. He described the enlightening evening and told how much he appreciated hearing about the work of the Holy Spirit to change Frank's life.

Suddenly, someone sitting several rows in front of me started waving his arms. It was John Florek. Many people were distracted by his wild gestures, including Pastor Armistead. No one interrupts the pastor when he is about to give a sermon. It's unheard of and, quite frankly, improper etiquette.

"John, is there something you want to say?" Pastor Armistead asked.

John nodded vigorously.

"Do you want to stand or come up here?"

John darted to the pulpit.

Pastor Armistead stepped back, clearly not knowing what to expect.

The congregation waited in anticipation for what was about to come out of his mouth.

"I certainly appreciated Frank Turner's message last night," he said respectfully. "But the talk Dr. Wolf gave yesterday morning at The Detroiter blew my socks off! His testimony radiated faith, trust, and hope in the Lord. He sincerely believes everything is going to work out. To me, that is complete trust."

Tears instantly filled my eyes. I was shocked at John's outburst. No one moved a muscle, waiting for his next words.

"Dr. Wolf reminded us to praise the Lord even when times are tough. He trusted God to get him through, and we should too. Dr. Wolf's faith is awesome, and it should be an inspiration to all of us. There's nothing else to say except praise God!" He lifted his arms.

As he stepped down from the pulpit and returned to his seat, scattered applause swept through the sanctuary. I wasn't expecting anyone to clap.

Some people turned and smiled at me. I was humbled and reminded that this was all about God's grace and power.

**Such confidence as this is ours through Christ before God.
Not that we are competent in ourselves to claim anything for
ourselves, but our competence comes from God.**

2 CORINTHIANS 3:4–5

This experience renewed my sense of God's purpose for my life. I had been given the privilege of reflecting his grace. I had shared my faith with a dedicated, godly group of men—serving as the Holy Spirit's voice.

Every day I continue to pray for God's guidance, wisdom, and leadership. I want to be his faithful servant. An open vessel for expressing his love and grace.

Being willing and able to reach out to others is a gift from God. He wants us to touch people's lives, whether we are with a group, a friend, or a stranger. Most often this happens one person at a time. God wants us to be his hands and feet, heart and spirit. Yet too many times we neglect his gentle nudges. We say we don't have time or we question if what we do really matters.

If any of this seems true for you, I want to remind you of a story I've heard told many times.[7]

There once was an old man who lived along the Atlantic coastline. He walked for miles along the beach each morning after the tide went out. Every so often, he would stoop down, gently lift something from the sand, and then toss it into the ocean.

One morning a curious neighbor followed him, trying to figure out what he was doing. It didn't take long to see that the man was picking up starfish, stranded by the retreating tide. He was throwing them back into the ocean so they wouldn't die of dehydration in the hot summer sun.

The neighbor laughed and called out in a sarcastic tone, "Hey, old man. This beach runs for hundreds of miles. There are thousands of starfish stranded here every day. Do you really think throwing a few back into the sea is making a difference?"

The man turned around, looking at the starfish he held in his hand. "Well, it makes a difference to this one, doesn't it?"

We are all starfish at one time or another, washed up on the beach of life's trials and tribulations. Yet Jesus is walking the beach to remind us that because of him, there is hope. He doesn't want us to die. He's there to pick us up when we fall, no matter what challenges or tragedies we face. What a great gift from God!

And there's more. He uses us to help others. We can be a blessing to people as he reaches out to them through our caring hearts, helping hands, voices of encouragement, prayers, and shoulders to lean on.

Saving a "starfish" is a wonderful way of giving and receiving the goodness of God.

> **I was hungry and you gave me something to eat, I was thirsty and you gave me something to drink, I was a stranger and you invited me in, I needed clothes and you clothed me, I was sick and you looked after me, I was in prison and you came to visit me. . . . I tell you the truth, whatever you did for one of the least of these brothers of mine, you did for me.**
>
> MATTHEW 25:35–40

We are not going to save the world, but we can make a difference by focusing on others. Influence one person or one hundred—every soul matters to God. He is the only safe haven for our future.

So don't give up. Keep seeking him. You'll find him through:

- His Word
- Prayer and meditation
- The encouragement of others
- Being a blessing to those in need.

Seek God because you love him.

Reach out to others because he loves you.

As the body without the spirit is dead, so faith without deeds is dead. JAMES 2:26

I believe God has selected every one of us to carry out his mission—to be his servant. No matter what our situations in life, he chooses each individual to perform a specific task for him. The trouble is, some people are not aware of his calling.

Tragedy has the potential to change that.

I thought I was aware before, but being in a wheelchair has made me more alert. In fact, I consider my wheelchair to be a real blessing. It makes me more visible and draws attention—for God's purposes! That doesn't make me special. I'm not suggesting he has singled me out to do anything more important than anyone else. What I am saying is, I'm unique and so are you!

God has given each of us special gifts in a one-of-a-kind combination to be shared in ways to glorify his name. He wants us to use these gifts at work, in the community, in our neighborhoods, and intimately among family and friends. This kind of service is more than general and generic—it is personal and specific.

By the grace of God, my adversity has made me stronger. It has given me an authentic and passionate gift of encouragement.

I have to admit, without my own personal tragedy I probably wouldn't be as eager to help others through their trials. The underlying needs of their situations wouldn't have even shown up on my radar. I've come to understand that having a "real life"—a godly life—means getting your mind off yourself and standing tall for God.

Although the Lord gives you the bread of adversity and the water of affliction, your teachers will be hidden no more; with your own eyes you will see them. ISAIAH 30:20

25

Training for the
Race of Our Lives

*Sometimes the greatest journey
is the distance between two people.*
W. SOMERSET MAUGHAM

Opportunities to help and encourage others continued to present themselves. One came disguised as a disappointment at first.

Skip had been working with me for over three years. I'd adjusted well to his requirements and he seemed to enjoy the challenges that came with me. His business grew rapidly, bringing more responsibilities. To ease the pressure, he hired additional instructors.

Following one of our routine sessions, Skip paused to talk with me about an important and difficult decision he'd made.

"Dr. Wolf, I've decided to give your Friday workout sessions to Edie Sherman starting next week." Edie was a new personal trainer with Body Specs. Our paths had seldom crossed, because we were at the gym on different days. "I trust her implicitly to do a good job."

I was shocked and disappointed, feeling as if Skip was abandoning me. I was also skeptical about working with someone new. But it was a done deal. I didn't have any say in the matter.

"I've already briefed her about you. I told her about your paralysis and your bike, including the part about it being off-limits to other clients. When I pointed out the plaque on the wall featuring that *News-Herald* article about you, she told me she couldn't wait to meet you."

Deciding it was in my best interest to give Edie a try, I agreed to meet her the following Friday. She approached me while I was on the bike.

"Hi, Dr. Wolf," she said with a warm smile. She seemed friendly and had an upbeat tone. Her body was lean and muscular, like an athlete's.

I reached out to shake her hand. "It's nice to meet you, Edie," I said politely but without enthusiasm. Still feeling disappointed by Skip, I was hesitant about working with her.

"Skip told me a lot about you. I love the idea of coaching an intensely focused, goal-oriented paraplegic."

She was clearly trying to make a good impression on me. But I remained skeptical. "Do you have experience with someone like me?"

"I've been an occupational therapist in the rehab unit at Saint Joseph Hospital in Ann Arbor, Michigan, for nine years. Most of my patients are victims of strokes, head injuries, or spinal-cord damage. A few need therapy after knee or hip replacement. Sadly, many lack motivation. They come to me because it's a requirement in their health-care plan, not because they want to improve. I got restless and burned out doing only that job."

"I've been around people who aren't self-motivated. I've never understood that mind-set."

"I also recently earned my master's degree in exercise physiology from Eastern Michigan University."

Her goal-oriented, competitive personality continued to spark my interest.

"After graduation, Skip's wife, who's a friend and colleague of mine, told me he was looking for a new employee. He offered me a part-time job, and I accepted."

"Why?"

"I needed a new challenge. Here I can help people with more than just basic functions. And this is a positive work environment."

I was impressed that she wanted other opportunities and wasn't satisfied with the status quo.

Was it coincidence that Edie and I were put together? Or divine direction? I still wasn't sure. "And what do you enjoy doing in your time off?"

Throwing the medicine ball with my personal trainer, Edie Sherman

"I'm a triathlete." Her face lit up. "After my first Ironman competition in 2002 at Lake Placid, New York, I raced the Navy Half Ironman in New Hampshire. That qualified me to represent the United States in the long-course world championship, Three-Quarter Ironman, in Sweden."

I didn't know much about the Ironman competition, but it certainly sounded impressive.

Without any instruction, she assisted me off the bike. We tossed the medicine ball back and forth for the remaining time of my training session.

When I got back to my office, I did some Internet research and learned that the Ironman is the most elite of the triathlon races. They have the longest distance of any competition, requiring a 2.4-mile swim, a 112-mile bike race, and a 26.2-mile run—a full marathon. If her goal had been to impress me, she'd succeeded!

As I worked more with Edie at Body Specs, I started asking her detailed questions, like "How do you train for these Ironman events?" and "What kind of bike makes the biggest difference in winning?"

THE GIFT IS YOU

Her responses were polite but extremely guarded. She clearly had doubts about my motives and didn't trust me.

But I loved hearing her elaborate on her experiences, especially in the exciting world of Ironman triathlons—something new to me. And her passion for competitive racing struck a strong chord with me. Over time, Edie recognized that my curiosity and interest were sincere.

As I expressed my pride in her accomplishments, Edie started feeling safe enough to open up to me. She told me that after completing many triathlon races from 2000 through 2004, she suffered severe lower back pain as a result of an inefficient bike and poor stretching habits. That made her tentative about her future.

Those feelings were compounded by her parents' attitude. They'd told her they wished she'd give up the demanding sport. This fed Edie's negative thoughts. She was seriously thinking about giving up her dream.

"What is your biggest goal?" I asked.

"To qualify for the 2008 World Championship Ironman in Hawaii. But I'd have to compete in the 2006 Ironman in Madison, Wisconsin, first. I don't know if I can even do that."

"That's a wonderful ambition. But it can never be accomplished if you don't believe in yourself. Are you going to bow down to the 'I can't' attitude, or are you going to press on?"

"I'm not sure."

Edie was a special person with unique talents—and unique needs. Her physical ability and drive were obvious, but one vital piece was missing: self-confidence. Her outer bravado camouflaged an undercurrent of inner doubts.

It became obvious that God had selected me to help her, even though she hadn't asked for it.

Our interactions required a delicate balancing act of persistence and sensitivity while I patiently waited for Edie to be receptive to my input. The social-work sidebar I got into when I was denied access to medical school the first time didn't derail me from my mission, as I'd thought. My educational roots taught me a lot about communication: how to be a good listener, how to make a difference through actions and interaction with people according to their needs, and how to write effectively.

These God-given tools equipped me to help people, both in and outside the realm of OB/GYN medicine. And they were exactly what I needed to make a difference in Edie's life.

Edie's job was to train me physically. Mine was to help her prepare mentally and emotionally to reach her goals. And I was up for the challenge! After all, I deeply related to Edie's dilemma. Ever since my accident, I'd been discovering how to overcome the emotional hurdles to success: all the anxieties, fears, and doubts that come with new, untraveled roads.

I couldn't count the number of times I'd doubted my abilities. But every time I faced stumbling blocks, God provided someone to lift me up. Dr. Krueger, sharing his presidential ring as a symbol of his confidence in me, and his phone call announcing my ACOOG vice-presidential nomination. Dr. Stanley, who found creative ways to preserve my energy, knowing how important it was for me to be fully prepared for the certifying board exam presentation. Time after time people had lifted me up when I doubted myself as I faced an uncertain future.

Now it was time to give back.

I wanted to do for Edie what others had done for me. Yet my mind, my time, and my energies were already filled with the responsibilities that came with being president of ACOOG. This was my third and final year in an executive capacity with the college. As usual, I had to carefully divide my resources to accomplish everything I longed to do.

When my term as president neared its end, Connie Hurn came to my mind again. I gave her a call.

"Would you be interested in helping me write a speech?" I asked. "I'll be giving it in March at the 2006 national ACOOG convention in San Antonio."

"I appreciate your offer. But I have no formal speech-writing experience."

"I'm confident you're the right person for the job," I said in my typical persuasive manner. "After all, you've been working with ACOOG for several years now. You know the organization. And you know me!"

Working with my writing partner, Connie Hurn, during one of our special interview sessions

"Thanks for your confidence in my ability, Dr. Wolf. I'd be honored to help you."

The two of us communicated often by phone and e-mail over the next few weeks. As our work on the speech neared culmination, Connie flew to Detroit to meet with me in person. After we discussed the final details, she hesitantly brought up a new subject.

"During my flight here, I had a dream," she said with a nervous laugh. "I dreamed we were writing a book together about your story of triumph over tragedy."

"That's amazing," I exclaimed, remembering my prayer that God would let me know when the time was right to ask her about this. "You may not believe this, but I was going to talk with you about helping me write a book about my story!"

We laughed at the "coincidental" timing. When she realized I was serious, she seemed to get even more nervous.

"I was only sharing my dream with you," she said, arms folded tightly over her torso. "I've never written a book."

"Well," I said with a grin, "you said you'd never had any speech-writing experience, but you've done a great job for me!"

I believed—without a doubt—that our paths had crossed through a divine connection for God's purpose. Our friendship was part of his providential plan for our lives.

I wasn't about to let her off the hook. After all, she had a dream, and so did I! This was no coincidence.

"You are the only person I want for the job," I told her—more than once.

After wrestling with God for more than a month, Connie finally committed herself to the project. I knew she would give 100 percent of her God-given talents.

My presidential speech went off without a glitch. It was a great conclusion to my three-year experience as an executive with the college. Throughout the convention, congratulatory handshakes, hugs, and comments from my colleagues reinforced my confidence in a job well done.

Four months later, Connie started traveling from her home in Fort Worth, Texas, to my home in Trenton, Michigan, to conduct monthly interview sessions for my book. Though reliving the accident and its immediate aftermath was painful, I enjoyed recalling all the ways, big and small, that God had worked in my life as a result.

When we got to the part about Edie, I could barely contain my enthusiasm about the upcoming Ironman race. "I definitely want this story in the book," I insisted.

Connie agreed.

"And I'll be able to tell you more about it after race day!"

"I can't wait to hear all the details the next time we meet," she said with a broad smile.

26

The Boomerang Effect

*There is no exercise better for the heart than reaching
down and lifting people up.*

JOHN A. HOLMES

As Edie's race day drew closer, I was more determined than ever to show my commitment to her. I asked Skip if I could put up a sign in the gym to cheer her on, and he replied with a resounding yes. With Frank's help, a twenty-foot banner was installed one week before the race. It said, "Good luck, Edie! Ironman Triathlon 9/10/06."

Anita and I made travel arrangements to attend the race. When I told Edie we were coming, she seemed dismayed.

"I won't be able to spend any time with you there. The race will keep me busy all day Sunday."

"No problem," I said. "If you have time on Saturday, maybe we could spend a few minutes together then."

"I'd like that," she replied with a big smile.

We did meet on Saturday. Knowing she had a lot on her mind, I was brief.

"Go out there and give it your best," I encouraged. Then I handed her a note to read privately before her big day. It said:

Dear Edie,

Many people talk and dream about competing, but only a few actually equip themselves to win. You are not just a dreamer. You have conditioned yourself for this race, physically and mentally. Nobody knows who will cross the finish line first. Yet all who prepare are winners.

Thank you for allowing the people who love you to be a part of your special day.

Good luck, my friend.

Sincerely yours,

David

Race day began with a miserable fifty-one degrees. The temperature hovered in the fifties from morning until night. And rain came down all day long. But that didn't stop the 2,439 Ironman competitors.

Edie competed in every leg of the race with great strength, focus, and endurance. She swam two and a half miles in the cold, white-capped waters of Lake Monona—against a headwind. She rode her bike 112 miles on slippery, wet pavement. Then she began the final leg of the triathlon: the twenty-six-mile foot race.

Anita and I hunkered on the sidelines, crowded in with thousands of other spectators. Our heavy raincoats kept us dry, but the air was still bone-chilling cold.

I couldn't see much from my wheelchair. But just being there was a thrilling experience. Edie's husband, Michael, followed her on his bicycle for most of the race and called my cell phone several times to give me her location on the course and a sense of her attitude.

As Edie rounded the first turn, I raised my fist high and cheered. She veered off the course and came over to hug me.

When she returned to running, I shouted, "Good luck, Edie! Keep going!" My own challenging experiences had taught me the value of being cheered on by others and the importance of not giving up.

Two hours later she rounded that same corner on her second lap. As she ran by me, she reached out and touched my hand.

"I'm proud of you," I yelled. I sensed her confidence and determination to continue the race.

Edie crossed the finish line in twelve hours, twenty-seven minutes,

Celebrating with Edie Sherman in the rain at the finish of her Wisconsin Ironman Triathlon race, September 10, 2006

and thirteen seconds—her personal-best time. She placed thirteenth in her division of 105 competitors!

After collapsing into the arms of her family, Edie looked around and found me. With tears of joy in our eyes, we hugged.

Before Edie returned to Body Specs, Frank and I hung another banner, saying, "Congratulations, Edie!" We also posted race photos on the gym walls. Memories of her victory gave everyone who came to the training facility a taste of Edie's success.

God placed Edie and me together for a reason. It was not a coincidence. He had planted the gift of encouragement in me long ago. But through Edie, I experienced the supreme value of that gift. This experience opened my eyes to the joy and gratitude we can receive when we serve others for God. It's what I call the Boomerang Effect. The more we live beyond ourselves, the more we experience his purpose for our lives.

THE GIFT IS YOU

Helping Edie brought me closer to God. That situation alerted me to be constantly on the lookout for ways to encourage others in need. It's become an integral part of my mission.

God permitted me to achieve success through the gifts of love, support, and encouragement planted in me by others. He plants those seeds in all of us. And he expects us to use them—often!

> There are different kinds of gifts, but the same Spirit. There are different kinds of service, but the same Lord. There are different kinds of working, but the same God works all of them in all men. 1 CORINTHIANS 12:4–6

– 172 –

27

Your Life Can
Make a Difference

It is one of the most beautiful compensations of life,
that no man can sincerely help another without helping himself.
RALPH WALDO EMERSON

While I was still wafting in the success of Edie's achievement, God gave me another assignment. It happened as I was listening to the Sunday morning message at church. He "tapped me on the shoulder" to get my attention. Then he spoke to me just as clearly as when I was in the hospital.

In the middle of Pastor Armistead's sermon, God's voice blocked out everything else in my mind. He said, "David, I want you to give a talk next year on May 6, 2007. The title will be 'Your Life Can Make a Difference.'"

The challenge inspired me, and I couldn't wait to share with Anita what the Lord had revealed to me.

But when I told my wife what happened, she reacted differently from how I'd expected. She was seriously opposed to my asking Pastor Armistead if I could give the message.

"Dave, it's one thing for him to invite you to give a talk. It's another thing for you to ask him. Sunday morning sermons are reserved for ordained ministers, not people who want to give testimonies. Are you doing this for yourself or God?"

Wow, that hurt! But I knew I wanted to do this for God, because his voice was vivid and filled my heart. Even Anita's position could not stop me from proceeding.

As soon as we arrived home from church, I went to my office and wrote to Pastor Armistead, telling him about my encounter with God.

Two weeks later I received a letter from him in response. "We would be delighted to have you speak to the congregation next spring on 'Your Life Can Make a Difference.'"

I was elated! I immediately began preparing a message.

My biggest challenge was figuring out exactly what God meant by the title. Good thing I had eight months to prepare—to pray, meditate, and dream about it. Quite the opposite from my last-minute experience at the truck stop!

I recalled something I'd told my children repeatedly over the years: "I don't know what you'll put on my tombstone when I die. But I really hope the inscription will say, 'His life made a difference.'" With that uppermost in my mind, the talk began to take shape.

In late October, Pastor Armistead was diagnosed with esophageal cancer, requiring an intense regimen of surgery, radiation, and chemotherapy. Much of his treatment was performed at the M. D. Anderson Cancer Center in Houston, Texas, where his son Paul was an oncologist.

His cancer kept Pastor Armistead away from the church for several months.

Though my friend had more important concerns than mine, I started to wonder whether he remembered his decision to let me speak to the congregation. So I wrote him a letter of encouragement.

Dear Pastor Armistead,

Anita told me you are back at M. D. Anderson to have your feeding tube removed. I hope all goes well. It is just one more step in your return to a normal life. I think of you often, and I pray for you every day.

As you might recall, I will be giving the 11:00 message on May 6, 2007. The title of my talk is "Your Life Can Make a Difference." God placed this message on my heart last September. I hope you can attend. It would not be the same without you being there. I really want you to pray with me prior to the talk and introduce me to the congregation.

Take care, dear friend. Remember, thousands of people, including me, are praying for you.

Love,

David

He sent an e-mail response:

David,

It's taking longer than expected to get over my surgery. The doctors are saying it could be a year before I feel normal again. But I'm planning on being there May 6th.

I cried when I read those words.

My pastor's commitment enabled me to become completely immersed in preparing my talk. It became a huge contributing factor to my deepened spiritual focus.

28

The Ripple Effect

You could call God's hand on you "the touch of greatness."
You do not become great; He becomes great through you.
BRUCE WILKINSON

May 6, 2007, arrived along with springtime in Michigan. The stage was set by the beauty of the season and the presence of my family in the pews. To my delight, my pastor came as well—his first time back at church after an absence of several months.

I took a position near the altar, adjacent to the choir. Pastor Armistead asked me where he should sit. I was surprised at his question, but motioned for him to sit beside me.

Appropriately, the service began with my favorite praise song, "Press On." Then Pastor Armistead approached the pulpit. In a quivering voice he gave his pastoral prayer, then sat back down for the next hymns, "It Is Well with My Soul" and "You Lift Me Up." He held my hand the entire time and choked back tears.

After Pastor Armistead introduced me, I moved to the center of the altar and looked out over the congregation. The pews were filled, shoulder to shoulder, with eager listeners. Their eyes spoke with expectation of a message of hope and comfort.

For a moment my nerves were a little raw. With a deep breath, I filled myself with God's presence and his confidence to deliver a message I prayed would be his.

I started with the title God gave me one year earlier to the day.

"Your life can make a difference. For some that may mean being a CEO of a large corporation. For others, it may mean becoming a world-class athlete. And for some, it may mean gathering a lot of wealth.

"James Dobson, from Focus on the Family, reminds us, 'Your successes will fade from memory too. That doesn't mean you shouldn't try to achieve them. But it should lead you to ask, Why are they important to me? Are my trophies for me or are they for Him? Those are critical questions that every believer is obligated to answer.'"[8]

At that point, I asked the congregation to bow their heads for prayer.

"Dear God, what a special day this is. We feel your presence in this room. We feel your love. I'm not sure why you chose me to give this talk today, but I am truly honored. I pray my words will be your words. I pray that what you've placed in my heart will turn people toward you. I pray my message will help people know you and bring them closer to you. Thank you for being with me now, Lord. Amen."

When I opened my eyes, I felt peaceful as I looked out over the people attending worship. They appeared calm as well. Silence filled the sanctuary. I paused for a moment, soaking in the Holy Spirit's presence before beginning my presentation.

"This morning I would like to talk to you about three men. The first is Job. Job was a man of God. He loved God. Job followed God in his heart every day of his life. Job had everything one would think was important: his family, land, and wealth.

"Then one day, Satan and God had a conversation about Job's life. Satan told God, 'The only reason Job is following you is because he is on top of the mountain. I guarantee he would curse you if he fell.'

"God told Satan, 'That is not true, and I will prove it. You can do anything to Job, but you can't take his spirit or his life.'

"Satan started destroying this man of God. He took his family. He took his land and his wealth. And he destroyed his health. Job had nothing left. Everything was gone except for one thing—God. Job never cursed God, and he never gave up.

"Of course, God knew what would happen. He gave his servant all the grace he needed to get through times of devastating hardship. Job's life made a difference, and it continues to make a difference to everyone who reads about him."

I noticed a few nods as I spoke those words. Some lips were pursed, and some folks had tears in their eyes. People were listening. I felt I had captured their hearts and emotions.

"The next man I want to talk about is the apostle Paul. Paul is one of my favorite people in the Bible. He was originally called Saul. Saul was a prominent Roman citizen and zealous in his persecution of Christians. As a matter of fact, he hated Jesus. But while he was on the road to Damascus, God struck him blind.

"God restored Saul's sight and transformed his life. After that he became known as Paul.

"Jesus wanted Paul to tell the world—including the Gentiles—about Christianity. Paul did everything in his power to carry out God's message. But he paid a high price for it. He was imprisoned. He was beaten and stoned. Yet even during his lowest times, he never gave up on the God he loved.

"Paul's life made a difference to the people of his day, and Paul's life continues to make a difference today."

I glanced slowly from one person to another while I talked. I wanted each person to feel a relational presence with me as I spoke. Like we were the only two people in the room. Faint smiles and intense eye contact reassured me that I had connected with the congregation. They were still listening.

"The last person I want to talk about this morning is me, David Wolf. Five and a half years ago, God used seven seconds of my life to make a difference.

"In April 2001, four months before my accident, I discovered the prayer of Jabez. Every night around midnight, after I finished seeing patients, I went down to the beautiful chapel in my medical building and prayed this prayer. I asked God to broaden my horizons. I asked him to take my life and use it in a fashion he'd never done before to carry his message to everyone I came in contact with. I prayed that prayer every night for three months."

After a brief description of my racing accident and the resultant injury, I shared stories about how God had used me to make a difference in people's lives. Laughter erupted when I mentioned The Detroiter talk and John Florek's passion about it. Tears streamed down cheeks when I described saving the little girl at the ballpark. And people nodded with approval when I shared Edie's success story. Their responses demonstrated the need for messages of hope, encouragement, and faith.

"God's love can be in your heart too. He has molded your hands to carry out the tasks that lie before you. As you do, he will walk by your side to give you inner peace.

"He has made each individual with the DNA, personality, and gifts we need to carry out his mission in our lives.

"God wants everyone to know he loves them. He wants everyone to follow him. But he has given us a choice.

"If you don't already know Jesus, I pray that you will get down on your knees and ask for forgiveness of your sins so you may receive his power and love. He will provide you with all the grace you need to make it through this troubled life. And when your time on earth is over, he will give you the gift of all gifts: eternal life. He has promised everyone who follows him a place he has prepared. When we are with him, there will be no more sorrow. No pain. No accidents. No cancer. No tragedy. We will live forever in joy and peace.

"Thank you, and God bless you." (Go to www.TheGiftIsYou.org to hear the entire presentation.)

Vigorous applause thundered throughout the sanctuary. Pastor Armistead led a standing ovation.

I wasn't expecting such an outward response to my talk. I couldn't hold back my tears of gratitude. I felt truly humbled.

As I shook Pastor Armistead's hand at the altar, I realized that my message had been choreographed by God. The congregation saw Jesus that morning, through Pastor Armistead's faith and mine. We became his face. The church witnessed him by seeing the hands of two men joined together in support of each other, men who had overcome adversity: one through cancer and one through paralysis. We became his Spirit in the flesh.

God's amazing love provided a spiritual feast for everyone present. It came through obedience to him by two men who drew attention and focus to him—together. The message wasn't about me. It wasn't about Pastor Armistead. It was solely about Jesus and the importance of obedience to God.

Whoever acknowledges me before men, I will also acknowledge him before my Father in heaven. MATTHEW 10:32

Following my talk, Pastor Armistead and I greeted those who came to the back of the sanctuary. Among them was Connie Hurn. It suddenly occurred to me that I'd been so caught up in preparing my talk that I never mentioned anything about her to my pastor.

After waiting patiently in line until it was her turn, Connie stepped forward and introduced herself to Pastor Armistead. "I really enjoyed being here today."

"Connie lives in Fort Worth," I added. "She's been helping me write my story. She travels here to Trenton once a month to interview me and others for the book. That's why she's in town this weekend."

"I appreciate you coming to hear David speak this morning," said Pastor Armistead. "What a nice surprise."

"Oh, it was my pleasure, I assure you." The beaming smile on her face confirmed her glowing words.

"Traveling here to do interviews must keep you very busy," the pastor said.

"It does. And I'll only be in Michigan for a short time. But I wonder if we might have a chance to meet while I'm here. Dr. Wolf has told me a lot about you. You've obviously played a key role in his life. I'd love to hear your perspective on his journey."

"I'd be delighted. Let me check my schedule. I'll be right back."

After Pastor Armistead left to consult his calendar, Connie turned toward me. "You know, this was the first time I heard about your experience with the Jabez prayer. I've been praying that prayer since 2001 myself. I did it because I wanted more purpose in my life. After hearing your talk today, I know in my heart that God wanted to begin enlarging my territory through a relationship with you."

"Unbelievable!" I exclaimed. "God sure knows how to bring people together." I felt truly blessed by his anointing of our work to honor him.

Never in my wildest imagination did I think my prayer would touch someone two thousand miles away. Someone who had been praying the same prayer. Someone who would become my writing partner for this book. Now, that's what I call enlarging a territory!

My talk and this brief encounter with Connie Hurn became the inspiration for Pastor Armistead's sermon two weeks later, on May 20, 2007. It was titled "Enlarge the Place of Your Tent."

Here is an excerpt from that talk, reprinted with his permission:

> Many of you are probably familiar with the prayer of Jabez, in which a man asked God to bless him and enlarge his territory. And by *territory*, Jabez probably meant his sphere of influence.
>
> Most of us want God to bless us and enlarge our territories. This is a legitimate request from Christians.
>
> One of the criticisms of the prayer of Jabez has been that it seems too self-centered—too focused on the individual. But I believe that when one man's territory is enlarged, many others' territories are enlarged as well.
>
> If you were with us week before last, at the eleven o'clock service, you heard Dr. David Wolf give his testimony. He talked about how the Lord has been

Pastor Duane Armistead, my spiritual mentor, delivering a sermon at First Presbyterian Church, Trenton, Michigan

blessing him since his go-kart accident six years ago, which left him paralyzed from the waist down. He wondered about his future, if any, as an OB-GYN physician.

But David Wolf's life has taken on new purpose and meaning. He is now involved in a ministry that involves telling others about the blessings of God even in the midst of a life-changing situation. He tells people that what the apostle Paul wrote in Romans 8:28 is really true: "In all things God works for the good of those who love him, who have been called according to his purpose."

This was the message Dr. Wolf brought to us two weeks ago. It is the message he continues to bring to all those who want to hear about the power of God to transform a tragic accident into a great victory for Jesus Christ.

During his talk, Dr. Wolf shared how he had been led to the prayer of Jabez. I am sure the Lord's answer to his request to enlarge his territory was not what he was expecting. But his accident has opened up new and exciting opportunities for him to tell others about the love Jesus has for them. His paralysis has indeed enlarged Dr. Wolf's sphere of influence.

God did not cause the accident. But he did work through the situation, giving Dr. Wolf new ways to share the gospel of Jesus Christ with others.

In this powerful sermon, Pastor Armistead gave everyone in the congregation two questions to think about:

What am I praying for?

Am I ready for God's answer?

The bigger question is: Are we content to sit on the sidelines, or are we beginning to venture into God's new territory for us?

Shortly after that morning, Pastor Armistead returned to his duties as senior pastor in the church. He started giving two sermons on Sundays with a high level of energy, confidence, and conviction in his voice. The congregation was pleased by his commitment to God and his church family.

Adversity can be a blessing. It holds potential for showing God's almighty power in our lives—power not only to heal us, but to help others through their challenges as well.

With God's sustaining grace, we can learn from our suffering. It can produce maturity and prevent us from falling into a pit of bitterness, resentment, or depression. His grace is our catalyst for growth. He gives us a chance to trust, express our faith, and grow in our relationship with him. This unmerited gift gives us greater humility and ability to become better Christians—better servants of God.

> **No temptation has seized you except what is common to man. And God is faithful; he will not let you be tempted beyond what you can bear. But when you are tempted, he will also provide a way out so that you can stand up under it.**
>
> 1 CORINTHIANS 10:13

My accident could have ended in depression, dropping out, or worse. Instead, I have become a better servant for God's glory. The result has been numerous occasions to share my testimony, including through this book. Talk about a ripple effect!

29

God Expects Humility

I am careful not to confuse excellence with perfection.
Excellence I can reach for; perfection is God's business.

MICHAEL J. FOX

Now more than ever, I find myself in unlikely places where God's gifts to me play out in my role with others. One situation started when I met Joan Drysdale. Shortly before my accident, she was hired to be the reception manager for my medical practice. The only time she saw me walk was during her initial interview.

Joan's first day on the job was the Monday after my accident. A thick blanket of emotions covered the office that day as the staff scrambled to reschedule patient appointments. Many spent time in the chapel, praying for my survival. No one knew if I was going to live or die, much less return to work.

Joan tried to ease the tension by demonstrating her faith and by jumping in to handle the scheduling nightmare. It was a challenging way to begin her job.

When I returned to work, my pace of life slowed down due to the wheelchair. That resulted in a greater focus and interest in the people around me, including my staff.

I was aware of Joan's martial-arts involvement when I hired her. But I had no idea of the extent of that commitment or the motivation behind such a disciplined lifestyle. At first, she was reluctant to talk about her life outside the office. A few jokes the staff had made about her interest in

"Karate Chops" kept her silent. But in my typically persistent manner, I was able to convince her of my genuine interest. In fact, she was amazed at the intensity of my listening skills.

Over the next several months, I made it a point to get to know Joan better. I discovered that in 1992, she and her husband, David, opened Drysdale's School of Tae Kwon Do in Riverview, Michigan. Their school became the first accredited ITF (International Tae Kwon Do Federation) school in southeastern Michigan. It was recognized for traditional training and had more than one hundred students, ranging in age from five to fifty-five.

Joan and David were highly recognized in the world of Tae Kwon Do. David was a master instructor with a seventh-degree black belt. He was respectfully known as Master David D. Drysdale Sr. VII Dan. He began his training in 1971 under the late Master Sang Kyu Shim IX Dan. He'd had the honor of training under the late father of Tae Kwon Do, General Choi Hong Hi. Joan was a senior instructor with a sixth-degree black belt and was respectfully known as Mrs. Joan M. Drysdale VI Dan. She was the highest-ranking female ITF instructor in the state of Michigan. She was one of only a few certified female ITF instructors in the USA.

As Joan shared this information with me, she could tell I was not only impressed but extremely proud of her accomplishments.

When I asked why she never told the staff about herself, she explained, "I don't like to brag. There's a fine line between arrogance and confidence."

Her genuine humility intrigued me. I checked out their website, www.drysdaleTKD.com. There I discovered the five tenets of Tae Kwon Do: courtesy, integrity, perseverance, self-control, and an indomitable spirit.

That fit Joan to a T.

Tae Kwon Do is not a sport—it's a way of life. First and foremost, Tae Kwon Do promotes love and devotion to God, expressed in Joan's school's mission statement: "What we do in life echoes into eternity." That obviously reflected what mattered most to Joan and David.

As I continued to learn about Tae Kwon Do, my understanding and respect grew for this highly disciplined way of life.

Over the next few months, Joan continued to share her accomplishments with me. Our talks led to two invitations, extended from Joan, for me to attend black-belt testing at their school.

The first time I went, I asked if I might be allowed to speak briefly to the students before they were evaluated.

"Normally only judges are given that opportunity," Joan replied. But she and David made an exception and granted my request. I was even seated at the judges' table. What a privilege!

Before the testing began, each of the three judges expressed appreciation for the work and dedication of the Tae Kwon Do students. Some black belts were also allowed to say a few words. Then Joan introduced me.

After thanking Joan, I turned toward the students and began my heartfelt message. "I'm proud to be a part of this important occasion today. It is truly an honor and privilege to witness your Tae Kwon Do accomplishments." My face flushed as I held back tears, remembering the support I felt when people cheered me on in the face of my challenges.

"As you begin your test, consider this food for thought. No matter what happens today, believe in yourself. Give it your best, regardless of what the judges decide. They will know it by your attitude and your confidence. Good luck!"

Talking to the group thrilled me. I loved having the chance to encourage them. And I felt respected as they maintained eye contact with me in my wheelchair.

Observing the students being tested humbled me. Seeing each one in action was the best education I could have received, resulting in a greater appreciation for Tae Kwon Do and the people dedicated to it. I realized that Tae Kwon Do is about more than simply mastering a set of physical techniques. Strength of character is on the line—something I'd dealt with a great deal since my accident.

The next time I was invited to another all-day event, Joan and David asked me to give a talk to the students before their test. Since I now knew what to expect, I was more excited than ever.

I had my act together a lot better this time, and I was able to speak with calmer emotions. I wanted to make a point about winning and losing, and I felt confident I could penetrate the hearts and minds of the students with one thought-provoking question.

"What is the difference between winners and losers? Losers quit when they're down, when they don't meet the mark, when they don't pass the test. Winners can fail, but they get back up, learn from their mistakes, and try again. Think about this today as you complete your tests. Good luck!"

Four students were being tested for a first-degree black belt: a nineteen-year-old woman, a twelve-year-old boy, and two men, ages thirty and fifty. The written test focused on knowledge of the patterns to be performed, Tae Kwon Do terminology, and the five tenets of Tae Kwon Do. The other testing components consisted of oral questions about martial arts and life in general, floor-exercise routines, and a demonstration of hand and foot self-defense techniques. It was amazing to watch the intense focus, precision, and determination of each student.

First-degree black belts were awarded after all testing was completed. Only one student did not pass: the twelve-year-old boy.

Joan allowed me to speak again. I congratulated the winners and expressed my admiration for their accomplishments. Then I turned to the student who did not receive an award and asked a revised version of my question. "How are you going to handle not receiving your black belt today? Are you a winner, or are you a loser?"

Without hesitation he answered, "I have failed this time, Dr. Wolf, but I'm not going to give up. I'm going to work on my skills and prepare for the next test."

I gave him a vigorous handshake and a broad smile. I wanted him to know I was proud of his confident yet humble response. After all, I knew what it meant to have the wind taken out of my sails, and I felt compelled to encourage this devoted student.

I was thankful to again be God's servant, honoring him with my small contribution. People are hungry for encouragement, especially when they're down. He knows whom to send to pick us up and put us on the right path.

The situation reminded me of Dr. Krueger's encouraging words when I was in the hospital at Saint Vincent's: "Two steps forward, one step back. Always remember to focus on the forward steps." He helped me earn my badge of humility.

The fear of the Lord teaches a man wisdom, and humility comes before honor. PROVERBS 15:33

The Drysdales planned a major ITF event for June 21, 2008. More than one hundred people from around the county attended. Some participated in the all-day testing of higher-degree black belts; others were there to watch. I was excited to be a part of such a meaningful, high-spirited activity.

Master instructor Robert Wheatley VIII Dan was there. He was the highest-ranking US ITF official, and he served as Secretary of Promotions and Discipline for the organization. He traveled throughout the world, leading Tae Kwon Do seminars. He was a role model, consistently emulating ITF integrity. His credibility gave him the privilege of judging students who aspired to high-degree black belts. His presence was an honor for this national-level event.

To my surprise, I was seated with Master Wheatley and other distinguished guests.

At the conclusion of the program, the Drysdales invited me to attend a dinner, along with all the judges. It was a gesture of appreciation for everyone's contributions to the day-long martial-arts event.

During the dinner, Master Wheatley asked me to come forward.

I had no idea what was in store. *Does he want me to speak? I wish he would have given me time to prepare.*

After I rolled up next to him, he announced, "Dr. Wolf, Master and Mrs. Drysdale have spoken to me about you. I've learned about your tragedy and the character you've demonstrated during the last seven years. You have maintained integrity as you rebuilt your life. I believe you are a role model for our organization because you exemplify the steadfast principles of the International Tae Kwon Do Federation. Therefore, I have made a decision taken very seriously by the ITF. It is my honor and privilege to award you an official first-degree black belt."

My eyes almost bugged out of my head!

Master Wheatley continued. "Only a few individuals with unique circumstances, who meet important criteria, are awarded this honor. Congratulations."

The moment seemed surreal as he handed me a black belt imprinted with my name in English and Korean. Next he gave me my own Tae Kwon Do uniform with an embroidered ITF logo. I was speechless as tears ran down my cheeks.

But I had to say something.

"I'm not often at a loss for words, but this is an unbelievable surprise. I'm overwhelmed and humbled by your confidence in me. I will continue striving for excellence, do my best, and always have hope for tomorrow. Thank you for this great honor."

Joan smiled as I returned to my place at the table, and David reached out to shake my hand. "Congratulations!" he called out. "Well deserved." Pleasant conversation and best wishes continued throughout the remainder of the dinner.

As we were all leaving the restaurant, Master Wheatley stopped me. He removed his black belt lapel pin and attached it to the lapel of my sports coat. "I want you to have this as a personal gift."

Again, I was stunned.

The moment felt similar to the time Dr. Krueger offered to give me his ACOOG presidential ring for encouragement and to express his confidence in my future. Only this time, the small pin was mine—permanently, to be worn proudly as a symbol of my accomplishments.

The recognition was spectacular, but also dangerous for a personality like mine. I remembered Joan's comment about the fine line between confidence and arrogance, and I couldn't help believing this was a test from God.

It also represented a valuable gift, the gift of self-awareness.

God's strategy for bringing me closer to him never ceases to amaze me. I found myself wanting to live up to the principles of Tae Kwon Do. But there was a choice to be made with this exciting recognition: be overzealous about my accomplishment, enjoying the accolades and attention—or practice humility.

I wanted to please God, and I did my best to pass his test.

Humble yourselves before the Lord, and he will lift you up.

JAMES 4:10

30

He Is Real

*Think about each person you meet each day of your life
and what effect you have upon them, for good or ill.*

BILL PORTER

The Tae Kwon Do experiences I had have proven to be another part of God's unsurpassed plan for my life. As the Master Builder, he worked in me through Tae Kwon Do—and especially through Joan—to liberate me from myself.

He's always been patient with me, understanding my exuberant personality. Even when faced with my flaws and weaknesses, he never gives up on me. Gradually he's infused me with a humble heart—which is necessary to glorify his name. Tae Kwon Do is one thing he used to accomplish this.

The challenge for me has been figuring out how to best serve God. There is a point to intentional planning when using our gifts. But there are also times when opportunity is spontaneous and when the way he wants our gifts to be shared with others catches us by surprise.

Following my accident, I was approved for Social Security disability and Medicare. After going back to work, I canceled those benefits and returned to my Blue Cross insurance. In the fall of 2008 I received a letter from Blue Cross stating I was required to use my Medicare insurance. I didn't think I had Medicare anymore since mine had been inactive for a long time. Confused by the information, I headed to the local Social Security office to clear up the dispute. I didn't really want to tackle the problem, but it had to be done.

I went there on a Friday afternoon after my Body Specs workout. I was in sweats, a Notre Dame sweatshirt, and tennis shoes, and I was sweaty. My hair was even a little bit messy—hard to believe for people who know me!

I got out of my van, rolled up to the entrance, and hit the automatic door button. When the door swung open, I was disappointed to see thirty people waiting to talk with someone. It was three fifteen, and I was concerned that I might not be able to get this matter settled by the time the office closed at four o'clock. But I was determined to resolve my situation.

A security guard sensed my hesitation and motioned me to a touch-screen computer, where everyone had to check in before getting help. There were seven categories. None of them seemed to match what I needed. I picked the seventh one. The number 25 came up, giving me my place in line. Great.

The security guard could tell I was frustrated. "Sir, can I help you?"

I told him my problem.

"Why don't you hit number two?"

I hit category 2 and the number 3 came up. *That's a lot better!* I thanked the guard, then parked my wheelchair and waited for a representative.

When my number was called, I explained my history and circumstances to an attentive rep. She clarified the Medicare requirements. I thanked her for putting my mind at ease. Then I turned around and rolled by the security guard on my way to the exit.

He started to follow me. I wondered if he just happened to be going my direction or if he thought I needed more help. *I got into this building by myself. I know how to get out.* Hoping he wouldn't bother me, I pushed the automatic button.

The door opened, and I rolled out. In the parking lot, the guard continued following me. As I neared my car, he asked, "Can I talk to you for a second?"

"Sure. What do you want?"

"I heard you talking to that rep about your go-kart incident."

"Oh. You want to talk about racing?"

"No. I'm interested in you. You're different. You seem special."

"What do you mean?"

"You're not like the others I've seen come in here. Whatever you have, I want it."

"You're kidding me."

"No."

"But you only saw me for thirty minutes."

"That's right. But I want to be more like you." His eyes told me he was serious.

"Well, there are two things that make me different from others."

"What are they?"

"First, I think you need to believe in yourself. I went from the top of the mountain to the bottom of the valley. But I came back up because I had faith it was possible."

"What's the second thing?"

"This is the most important one. You need to believe in Jesus Christ. I'm different, special, because of him."

"What an interesting statement."

I could tell I had his undivided attention, so I continued. "If you put your faith in Jesus, your whole life will be different. He's there for you, just as he is for me. If you accept him as your Savior, he will walk by your side every day. He will be with you in your darkest moments, and he will carry you as far as the road travels."

Tears filled his eyes. "My life has been heading in a downward spiral. Nothing has been going right. Everything is falling apart. To be honest, there are times I just don't want to go on living."

"But today, you met me. And now you know what to do. Just believe in Jesus. Make sure he is in your heart every day. And always believe in yourself." I loved having the opportunity to encourage someone who had lost hope.

With a vulnerable tilt of his head, he concluded, "I think you were supposed to come into my life today. I needed to hear your message."

"You know, you're special too. You didn't have to help me today, but you did. You went out of your way to make a difference for me."

"I guess I did, didn't I? Thank you."

We shook hands and looked into each other's eyes for a moment. Then we went our separate ways.

I felt humbled by this encounter. I didn't get his name. He didn't get mine. But I was sure of one thing: God was present.

I rolled over to my van with a smile. *God did it again!*

In that moment, I wasn't Dr. Wolf. I wasn't president of ACOOG. I wasn't even a Tae Kwon Do black belt. I was just a man in a wheelchair, making a difference for another man. I was a servant of God—and I was grateful.

We never know how or when God is going to use us. But if we have a faithful relationship with him, we will be ready for the task.

Dear children, let us not love with words or tongue but with actions and in truth. 1 JOHN 3:18

It's not up to us to know how God will see us through when adversity strikes. What matters is our response, knowing his love will be enough. Our trials will always be matched by God's undeserved kindness, his grace. Our job is to be open to it by trusting and obeying him, and always giving him all the praise. If we truly believe this, we will replace asking him, "Why?" with praying, "I know you are here for me. Help me listen, be patient, and follow your plan for my life."

When we fill ourselves with his grace—the gift of all gifts—we can be a significant expression of it to others. We can serve as a beautiful hue in his rainbow of grace to match the color of our trials and the hardships of others. Each hue is important and has potential for bringing people closer to Jesus.

No one can be the whole rainbow, but each of us can express one of the beautiful colors—for him. We can shepherd and assist others who need support. We can encourage, inspire, and motivate.

As we give away the gifts God has given us, we will bring glory to him. Our lives *will* make a difference.

The body is a unit, though it is made up of many parts; and though all its parts are many, they form one body. So it is with Christ. For we were all baptized by one Spirit into one body—whether Jews or Greeks, slave or free—and we were all given the one Spirit to drink.

> **Now the body is not made up of one part but of many. If the foot should say, "Because I am not a hand, I do not belong to the body," it would not for that reason cease to be part of the body. And if the ear should say, "Because I am not an eye, I do not belong to the body," it would not for that reason cease to be part of the body. If the whole body were an eye, where would the sense of hearing be? If the whole body were an ear, where would the sense of smell be? But in fact God has arranged the parts in the body, every one of them, just as he wanted them to be. If they were all one part, where would the body be? As it is, there are many parts, but one body.**
>
> 1 CORINTHIANS 12:12–20

Many people find it hard to believe in God because we cannot see him or touch him. But God is not a mirage. I know he is real because I feel his presence. He walks by my side every minute of every day. I see him with the eyes of my heart.

In the early spring of 2010, Anita and I went to Florida for a dear friend's retirement dinner. We had a few hours to kill before our return flight to Trenton, so we stopped at a shopping center near the Orlando airport. After looking around for a while, we sat on a bench outside the mall. It was a warm, breezy spring day—perfect weather for being outdoors. Anita read a book while I enjoyed a little people watching.

Across the parking lot, three empty buses pulled up to the shopping-center entrance adjacent to where we were sitting. The bus doors opened, and ramps with cages lowered hydraulically. Figuring they must be for handicapped people, my radar went up.

Moments later, about fifteen adults came out of the shopping center, pushing children in wheelchairs. Before they reached the buses, someone asked, "Does anyone want ice cream?"

"Yes!" the children screeched.

A few of the chaperones marched back into the mall and returned with cones.

Some of the kids were so severely handicapped they couldn't feed themselves. But with cheerful voices, gentle hands, and loving hearts, the chaperones made sure every child enjoyed a cold, creamy treat.

God's gift of joy was written all over those messy faces. His grace was evident in the work he was doing through the chaperones.

I guarantee that every one of those adults had problems. Yet their own adversities didn't stop them. Each of them had received God's love and naturally poured it out to those kids.

Some passersby looked uncomfortable when they saw the group of handicapped children. But those who had eyes to see witnessed God in action that day!

A gift opens the way for the giver and ushers him into the presence of the great. PROVERBS 18:16

As Anita and I left for the airport, I praised God. He did it again! Observing these adult helpers confirmed my faith in the presence and power of his Holy Spirit.

31

But God . . .

Don't cry because it's over.
Smile because it's happened.
DR. SEUSS

God blessed me with thirty-one years of providing women's health care. But in June 2010, a few months before I turned sixty-three, unsettling thoughts began to plague me. *Is it time to give up my God-given passion? Should I retire? If so, what's next?* Like a broken record, the questions repeated themselves, day and night.

Anita, Raquel, Brad, and my precious grandchildren were on one side of the equation. The idea of more time to relax and hang out with family was enticing. Patients and residents were on the other side of the equation. So much of my identity was tied up in being an OB/GYN physician. How could I stop living the dream I'd had since I was nine years old?

Anita deserved my time, energy, and devotion to family. Yet I couldn't imagine a future without OB/GYN medicine. It was a dilemma God and I had to work out together. So I prayed incessantly about the choice confronting me.

Please, Lord, show me the way. Help me make the right decision. Help me embrace a future led by you. Help me commit to your will. Direct my steps and keep me stable.

I had learned through the years to rely on prayer to provide relief during the waiting period. It was my only weapon against Satan's deceptive lies. But, as in many times in the past, God's answers did not come easily or quickly.

Be still before the Lord and wait patiently for him.

PSALM 37:7

Patience was crucial. Yet my emotions tried to get the better of me. (No surprise there, based on my past behavior.) Anxiety crept in every day. I'm sure Satan enjoyed my confusion and stress.

But God knew my heart. I'd always loved doctoring. And my mission work in Haiti, followed by years of practicing OB/GYN medicine from a wheelchair, had prepared me for new opportunities to serve him. I knew he wasn't through with me yet. My gifts were still needed.

In his divine way, God used others—as he had many times before—to help steer me in the right direction.

One evening in November, after a late supper, Anita waited for me to get comfortable in my recliner before sharing some news. "We received an invitation from the hospital in the mail today. They're having a fund-raiser for the Wyandotte Clinic for the Working Uninsured." She handed me the brochure.

I barely glanced at it. The thought of trying to maneuver through a crowd of people who were standing around socializing and eating hors d'oeuvres made me cringe. It wasn't easy for me to mingle from a wheel-chair. A sit-down dinner would have been easier. "I really don't want to go." I set the brochure on an end table.

"You might be surprised to learn what they're doing. And I think you'd enjoy the program."

"I'd rather just make a donation."

"Well, think about it. We don't have to RSVP right away. You've got a couple of days to decide."

Anita was wise to spark my curiosity and then put the idea on the back burner. She knew me well!

There was no real reason not to go. My practice was winding down. I was only seeing patients two days a week. I had the time. I just didn't feel like going.

Anita didn't say another word to me about it. But that invitation on the end table kept reminding me of the decision I needed to make. And God was nudging me to say yes.

A day before the RSVP deadline, Anita asked, "Have you made up your mind?"

"I'll attend if you go with me."

"Of course I'll go!" I knew Anita was doing her best to plant meaningful seeds for my future opportunities.

The well-attended event was held at the Henry Ford Health Center–Brownstown Facility. Rolling around was even more difficult than I anticipated, even with Anita's help. The refreshment area was especially crowded with people shaking hands and talking about the impact of Michigan's unemployment crisis on the medical arena. I joined in the conversation enough to be polite. But I was really uncomfortable.

When Dr. Chris Bush, medical staff president for Henry Ford Wyandotte Hospital, approached the podium to give a talk, everyone took a seat—putting them all on my level. Much better!

"The number of uninsured working adults in this country continues to grow," Dr. Bush said. "Southeastern Michigan and metropolitan Detroit have been more severely impacted than most areas due to our industrial and manufacturing environment. As jobs vanish and more businesses are forced to cut back on expenses, health-care coverage continues to diminish."

I was well aware of the situation. Several of my patients had no insurance coverage. This speech was a painful reminder of the financial strain being put on them and thus on my medical business.

"Due to the emergent health-care crisis, national and state initiatives are being developed to provide assistance for the uninsured. Yet the need is not being answered on the local level."

I could hardly wait to hear their solution to the problem.

"Addressing health care for the growing uninsured population has become a priority for the Henry Ford Health System. The intention of the Wyandotte Clinic is to provide appropriate and prompt primary and preventive care to help decrease the burden on local hospital emergency rooms before medical needs become acute. That care is delivered to patients by volunteer doctors, nurses, and other medical personnel who donate their time to help the community."

That got my attention. This could be a great solution for my patients with no insurance. "This is an excellent opportunity for you, as medical professionals, to help the community you live in to thrive."

Those words lassoed my heart. I wanted to be a part of this!

I glanced at my wife and gave her a wink of gratitude. She responded with a knowing smile. Anita hadn't stopped believing in God's plan for my life. And she'd sensed this was something I would love doing. What a clever woman!

On the way home, I bombarded her with one-way conversation. Filled with excitement, I was already visualizing my new schedule. "I'm only seeing patients at my office two days a week, so I could volunteer at least one day. And this could be a great opportunity for my residents too. They need to learn the importance of volunteer work in the community."

"Hold on just a minute." She chuckled. "Don't you think you should make up your mind about retirement before you start adding more to your schedule?"

Her logical comment reminded me I still had a major decision to make.

When we got home, I called Brad. After sharing the highlights of the evening with him, I asked, "Think you could help me figure this thing out?"

"Sure, Dad. How about I come over on Saturday? We can sit in the garage, smoke a cigar, and think this through." Smoking cigars together in the garage had been a tradition for Brad and me whenever wise counsel was needed.

He arrived mid-afternoon. After a long hug at the front door, we moved to the driveway. He opened the garage door, pulled up a lawn chair, and sat next to me.

"Thanks for coming," I said.

"No problem. Glad to be here."

After lighting the cigars, we sat in silence for a few moments, contemplating.

"There's going to be a big transition when I retire," I said with some hesitation.

"It will definitely be a major adjustment."

"I'm trying to figure out what I'll gain or lose by retiring. I have serious reservations about giving up my practice—and my medical building." Tears threatened to choke my voice. "I just can't seem to get a handle on it."

"Whether you're sixty-three or eighty-three, it will never be easy saying good-bye to your work. But if you do retire, your patients would be transferred to your partner. And you trust him, right?"

"Completely."

"And that would allow you to help the people at the free clinic more often. Sounds like they need you more."

Brad's message was exactly what I needed to hear. And he made it sound so simple.

"I think it's time, Dad."

"I think you're right."

As the sun began to set, we ended our man-to-man conversation and emptied the ashtray full of cigar ashes and stubs.

I rolled up the garage ramp into the house, ready to share my decision with Anita. I had no doubt in my mind God had spoken to me through Brad, confirming that this was his way of moving me forward.

> Whoever sows sparingly will also reap sparingly, and whoever sows generously will also reap generously. Each man should give what he has decided in his heart to give, not reluctantly or under compulsion, for God loves a cheerful giver. And God is able to make all grace abound to you, so that in all things at all times, having all that you need, you will abound in every good work. As it is written: "He has scattered abroad his gifts to the poor; his righteousness endures forever." 2 CORINTHIANS 9:6–9

The next day, I started sharing heartfelt good-byes with my colleagues. Every day I cried with patients as I shared the news of my decision to retire.

By June, instead of feeling ready to move on, I was buried in mournful emotions. After my office furniture and my special exam table were moved to the new clinic, seeing the empty room pierced my heart even deeper.

On the last Friday of June, as I rolled into my office for the last time, I prayed. *Please, God, give me courage to do this new season of my life well.*

That evening, an open house at my office gave my patients a chance to say farewell and express their gratitude to me. Tender hugs and long handshakes spoke our raw emotions with sincerity.

As I prepared to make my final exit, I choked out a few words. "You have been more than staff to me. You've been family. I will miss you and always treasure the years we spent together. The time we've shared has been a great gift."

In an attempt to lighten up the mood a bit, I added, "Remember, you're welcome to volunteer with me at the Wyandotte Clinic any time!"

Tentative smiles appeared on the many sad faces.

Everyone huddled around the entrance as I rolled down the ramp to the parking lot for the last time. I waved to them all before getting into my van.

Once situated and alone, I put the key in the ignition. But instead of starting the engine, I sat there and bawled like a baby. A river of tears soaked my shirt. I felt numb and exhausted.

When I lifted my head, I saw the plaque on the wall of the building. It reminded me of my purpose here. This practice was, above all, dedicated to God. My tears ceased.

Thank you, Lord, for allowing me to serve you in this special place. Thank you for the gifts given by every person who has entered this beautiful building. I hope you are pleased with what has been accomplished here. Please be with me on the next steps of my journey.

Memories flooded my mind. Decades of meeting with patients had left an indelible mark on my heart. Friendships had been forged here. This was where I met Frank. We had poured ourselves into the construction of this building and became lifelong friends as a result. The one-of-a-kind chapel was a miracle orchestrated by God. In this place, my worth had been assured, my pride exposed, humility developed, and maturity gained. My purpose had been revealed here.

As I drove away, a tremendous sense of gratitude washed over me.

Bringing closure to this chapter of my life was a painful challenge. But I knew beyond a doubt that God would be with me in my season of retirement just as much as he had been all along.

To make it official, I wrote an article for *The News-Herald.*

A Message of Appreciation and Gratitude
From Dr. David Wolf to all of my patients

When I was nine years old, I dreamed about becoming a doctor. What a blessing it's been to have my dream come true here in the Downriver community. Although I will continue serving as director for the OB/GYN residency program at Henry Ford Wyandotte Hospital, the time has come for me to retire from my medical practice.

This has been a difficult decision because I enjoy being an OB/GYN physician and I love my patients. My heart has been dedicated, as stated on the bronze plaque outside the entrance of my medical building, "to God and the caring of women and their unborn babies." However, the Bible reminds us, "There is a time for everything, and a season for every activity under heaven" (Ecclesiastes 3:1).

It is time!

Words cannot express what you have meant to me during the years as your physician. Every one of you has made an unforgettable difference in my life. I hope I made a difference in yours as well. Precious memories of our time together will sustain me as I follow God in a new direction, which will include volunteer work at the Wyondotte Clinic for the Working Uninsured. (To learn more about the clinic, go to www.TheGiftIsYou.org.)

In closing, I want to leave you with words from George Bernard Shaw:

I am of the opinion that my life belongs to the community, and as long as I live it is my privilege to do for it whatever I can. I want to be thoroughly used up when I die, for the harder I work the more I live. I rejoice in life for its own sake. Life is no "brief candle" for me. It is a sort of splendid torch which I have got hold of for the moment, and I want to make it burn as brightly as possible before passing it on to future generations.[9]

It is time to pass the torch!

Please accept my deepest gratitude and appreciation for the privilege of serving as your OB/GYN physician.

Sincerely,

David L. Wolf, D.O., FACOOG

But God wasn't ready for me to pass the torch.

After developing a routine at the new clinic, I saw needs beyond gynecological care. People needed encouragement and hope. They needed God's grace. In addition to serving as a volunteer physician, I could reach into their hearts. Many times I prayed with people and talked to them about Jesus. The Wyandotte Clinic became my Haiti.

My work was still dedicated to God.

Serving as a volunteer physician at the clinic became my God-given inspiration to establish a virtual health-care community known as The Center for Women's and Children's Health and Well-Being. It functions as a conduit for providing medical, psychological, and social resources to improve and sustain the health and well-being of women and children in Michigan. I am proud to chair this network. (For more information, visit www.TheGiftIsYou.org.)

I believe—beyond a doubt—that prayer, people, and passion are gifts from God. Prayer has power and gives us hope if we trust God. People are meant to be a reflection of Jesus, to love, encourage, and support one another. And passion has purpose when it is led by God.

I do not waver in these beliefs.

Jesus said, "Did I not tell you that if you believed, you would see the glory of God?" JOHN 11:40

32

The Ride of My Life

*We are never more fulfilled than when our longing
for God is met by his presence in our lives.*

BILLY GRAHAM

As much as I need air to breathe, I need my wheelchair to live. It has been a great and unexpected gift—the ride of my life! It has helped me appreciate God more, thank him more, and touch more lives for him. It has been a springboard to a future I would never have dreamed possible.

My daughter, Raquel, summed it up perfectly when Connie interviewed her for this book in 2011.

> My father was a workaholic and didn't take time to "smell the roses."
> I've often wondered if the accident, while leaving him incapacitated
> in some ways, in other ways saved his life.
>
> Paralysis can leave a person with a sense of hopelessness and a
> devalued life. But I think it has made my dad's life better.
>
> He was used to going ninety miles an hour on the racetrack of
> life. God knew it was time for him to slow down. Dad wasn't going
> to do it on his own. Something dramatic had to be done. God
> temporarily pulled the plug and reset the circuit.
>
> The end result is what you see today: a man more available to
> do God's work.
>
> Do I wish the accident had never happened? Of course! Do I

wish I could turn back time and restart his metaphorical ninety-mile-an-hour sprint through life? Absolutely not.

While he only has use of half of his body, I believe he is more whole now than ever before.

Life is not where we have been—disappointments, hardships, or crises. It's about where we are going and how we handle the circumstances we have been given.

The real competition in our unpredictable journey is striving for and reaching God's finish line.

Be joyful always; pray continually; give thanks in all circumstances, for this is God's will for you in Christ Jesus.
1 Thessalonians 5:16–18

I do not know where my story is going to end. I don't know when it will end. But one thing I do know: God will continue to give me courage and confidence to press on because he loves me. He will not allow my wheelchair to prevent me from making a difference.

My prayer for you, dear reader, is simple yet profound. I pray you will be inspired by the joy and peace God has given me.

If you are a Christian, I pray you will rededicate your life to God, that you will pray more diligently and more often.

If you don't know Jesus Christ, I pray you will accept him as your Savior today. Don't wait until tomorrow. Tomorrow may never come.

His hands are stretched out for you as he says, "Come, follow me."

Here I am! I stand at the door and knock. If anyone hears my voice and opens the door, I will come in and eat with him, and he with me. Revelation 3:20

Once you have accepted Christ as your Savior, his gifts will flow freely in and out of your heart. And the promise of his greatest gift will always be waiting for you—the gift of eternal life. Don't reject this gift of all time. Once the call of God comes to you, follow him. Never stop receiving him, and never stop giving out the gifts he has given you.

Making Christmas memories with my family. (Back row L-R : Raquel, Marc; middle row: Abby, Anita, Sawyer, Beth, and Brad; front row : Tyler, Noah, me, and Grayson)

> **Each one should use whatever gift he has received to serve others, faithfully administering God's grace in its various forms.** 1 PETER 4:10

My accident became the catalyst for telling a story based on God's messages to me while I lay in a hospital bed, fighting for my life. Without him, my story would have no power at all.

Tragedy struck me like a bolt of lightning. Until then, my life was out of balance and filled with distractions. Although I've always had a strong Christian faith, a lot of my focus was on worldly things and outward appearances: cars, clothes, accomplishments, and more. Too many times I put myself first, not realizing the impact my personality and decisions could have on the people who love me the most.

My accident slowed me down enough for God to get my attention. My faith and character were tested to the core. Yet over time my tragedy has made me a better man. If I live the rest of my life in a wheelchair, I won't be disappointed.

You might have the most expensive car, a closet filled with designer clothes and shoes, the biggest house in the neighborhood, a powerful job, and a cabinet filled with trophies and awards. All of these could bring you fame, fortune, and attention. But none of it matters without Jesus in your heart. You may be a winner to the world, but being in service to God is what counts.

When Jesus comes into our lives, real miracles start happening—miracles of the heart, mind, and spirit. He is the only one who can set you on a course to real life and fulfillment.

We all face difficulties. Some are short-lived. Others may last a life-time. I would rather be remembered as a man of God who made some mistakes yet pressed on than someone who gave up on himself and the power of our Lord and Savior.

The love, peace, and contentment I have been given since my accident is beyond understanding. I do not worry about my disability. Instead, I focus on all the possibilities of life in him.

I have learned that God is no less God when adversity changes our plans. Nothing catches him by surprise. We can only discover this truly by allowing Jesus to walk by our side through all the good and bad days of our lives.

Each of us has a story. And every life includes trials. But not everyone has a close walk with Jesus. I hope my story leads you to reflect on the value of prayer, humility in his grace, confidence in his Word, and appreciation for the gifts others have given to enrich your life.

God will never let you down. He makes a difference so your life can make a difference.

I am in awe of our heavenly Father. The gift is *him!*

God bless you.

David

Consider it pure joy, my brothers, whenever you face trials of many kinds, because you know that the testing of your faith develops perseverance. Perseverance must finish its work so that you may be mature and complete, not lacking anything.

JAMES 1:2–4

Posing with my residents at their graduation

*Giving a heartfelt speech at my
residents' graduation*

*A special evening for Anita and me at the Henry
Ford Wyandotte Hospital OB/GYN Residency
Program graduation, June 1, 2013*

Appendix 1

My Father

by Brad Wolf

My father stands ten feet tall to me. In reality he is only 5 foot 7 inches, but his heart is twice the size of his body. He is stocky and fair skinned, with dark graying hair. His smile lights up the room, and you can see his soul when you look into his eyes. He wears a mask of confidence, but he doesn't let that get in the way of people seeing his real face. The best quality about him is that he wears his heart on his sleeve.

All of these things don't even shed a light on all of my father's good qualities. His job is to help people, and in a way to create miracles. You see, my father is a doctor. He delivers babies. He treats his patients as if he has known them all of his life. He doesn't just give them medical help; he does his best to help them with all of their problems.

I think the world of my father. Other people do too.

For example, my family and I go out to eat every Sunday. It isn't a surprise when one of Dad's patients comes to our table and says, "Hi, Dr. Wolf. Is this your family?"

"Yes. This is my wife, Anita, and these are my two kids, Brad and Raquel."

Many times a patient will turn to my sister and me and say, "You are lucky to have such a good father. He is a very good man."

Raquel and I smile and say, "Yes, we know. Thank you." We don't think much of it, because this kind of thing happens regularly. I know that my father must have touched people's lives greatly to be complimented so often.

People respect my dad for who he is, not for what he does. He goes out of his way to help many of his patients. For instance, he has office hours until two in the morning on most nights and usually works about fifteen hours a day because he cares and listens to his patients' medical and personal concerns. He even has a chapel in his office in case he or his patients need to turn to God for help or support.

My dad cares so much about being an OB/GYN physician that he travels to Haiti with a group of doctors every year to help the people there. Haiti is a third-world country. The Haitian government doesn't appreciate Americans coming into their country. But my dad goes anyway.

Haiti is not a desirable place. Chances are high for getting malaria. The doctors can't eat the food or drink the water. During the week that my father is there, he only eats three granola bars a day. That's it.

My father looks forward to the Haiti trip every year in hopes of helping at least one person, no matter how uncomfortable or dangerous it is to go there. When he comes back from his trips, he's always a changed person and full of stories.

His favorite story is about the time he and a guide hiked up a mountain to a house where a lady was having a baby. The trail was rocky and steep. It was hard to believe that anyone lived up there. However, he got there and delivered the baby successfully.

The parents of the child were so grateful they asked my father to name the baby. These people didn't know my father, yet they trusted him to name their newborn. He was honored and named the baby Sue.

My dad is a great doctor, but he is an even better father.

He works long hours and isn't home very often. As a result, I don't get to see him that much. Yet I always know he is thinking of our family. Whenever he has a free minute at the office, he calls home to see how things are going. Sometimes he'll leave a note on my bathroom mirror that says, "Have a good day! I love you." It reminds me that he's always thinking of me. I've never thought, *I wish Dad were here,* because he's always with me when I need him.

There was one special time in my life that I thought he was going to miss. It was about two years ago, when my hockey team was in the state playoffs. This was a pretty big deal to me. My father had to go out of town for a hospital conference the weekend of the tournament. I didn't like him being gone, but I figured there was nothing I could do about it.

I played the first game. And we got beat ... bad. My dad called shortly after I got home. I told him we lost. He said, "Well, you're going to have to win the next two games then!" The tournament was a two-game knock-out, but we still had a slim chance to win. "You can do it, Son. I'll see you tomorrow." Then he hung up. I didn't understand why he was so abrupt. But I blew it off.

We had to play two games the next day. I showed up wishing my father could be there. When I stepped onto the ice for warm-ups, I looked into the arena corner where he always stands. And there he was, smiling and giving me that special look that said, "You can do it!"

Seeing him was a surprise. He'd dropped what he was doing to come home and watch me play hockey. Having him there meant so much to me.

It was an especially good thing my dad was there, because my face got cut during the game. He put ten stitches in my chin so I could continue to play. The look in his eyes told me that he was proud of me for scoring the goal and for continuing to play when I was hurt.

We ended up winning the game, and I scored the winning goal.

Unfortunately, we lost the next game by one goal. It was disappointing. But when I looked in the corner, I saw my dad standing there, still yelling, "You can do it!"

My father has made a great impact on my life. His priorities are straight. He is kind to everyone, and he is always helping people. Most of all, he is there for his family.

My dad is a great father. He is my role model.

Appendix 2

"Cuts Hurt Paralysis Rehab"

Courtesy of *The Detroit News* Archives
Published on Sunday, September 30, 2001

DETROIT—Advances in technology mean the odds of surviving a spinal cord injury suffered in a diving accident or car crash look brighter now than ever before.

But even if they have medical insurance, those who suffer traumatic injuries face an uphill battle getting long-term physical therapy, equipment and medication.

Cost-cutting efforts have led to quicker discharges from hospitals and inpatient rehabilitation facilities, which critics say can require new hospital stays and even prove fatal.

It's an issue that pits rehabilitation professionals against an increasingly competitive managed-care industry. As insurers limit coverage for long-term care needs, doctors are left to grapple with difficult decisions.

Complications after a hasty discharge can wipe out any savings from sending a patient home early, some doctors argue. And in extreme cases, the trend can shorten the lifespan of those initially saved by the best technology modern medicine has to offer.

- 217 -

"People are now finding their insurance companies are ill-equipped or unwilling to provide them what we in the business believe are appropriate goods and services," said Dr. Edward Nieshoff at the Detroit Medical Center.

Nieshoff, who treats spinal cord injury patients, is himself paralyzed below the waist from a 1978 diving accident. He bristles while describing changes in care since his injury.

While he spent a month in inpatient rehabilitation following his injury, most patients with similar injuries now are allowed an average of two weeks.

"Improvements in emergency care have increased the number of people who survive," said Nieshoff, medical director of Spinal Cord Injury Services. "The problem that arises is that with people saved comes therapy and rehab"—which can be costly.

"The irony in all of this is we do such a fantastic job in saving people and then we essentially cast them aside because their follow-up care is expensive and their insurance companies are held to the lowest possible standard."

Shortened treatment time also dismays Dr. Michael DeVivo at the University of Alabama, where he directs the National Spinal Cord Injury Statistical Center.

"Mortality rates have started going up," he said. "Is it because of managed care? I don't know, but it's a disturbing trend that wasn't there before."

DeVivo refers to data from rehabilitation institutes nationwide that show death rates for people surviving more than a year after their injury—which had decreased since the 1970s—have begun to rise.

The death rate dropped from 1973 to 1992, but climbed 33 percent between 1993 and 1998 among those with spinal cord damage who survived at least a year.

Susan Pisano, spokeswoman for the American Association of Health Plans—which represents about 1,000 health plans nationwide—agrees that long-term care needs attention.

"Over the past five or 10 years, we've had little or no discussion about what benefits should be covered," she said Saturday. "Very broadly speaking, on a policy level, the area of long-term care does need some attention. Here you do have a situation where we have changing needs."

Type of care varies

The type of care varies greatly between people who are injured in auto accidents—who Nieshoff says receive "exemplary coverage"—and those who rely solely on commercial insurance.

Under Michigan's no-fault insurance law, which set up a catastrophic claims fund to cover long-term care, someone paralyzed as a result of an auto accident qualified for insurance-paid home modifications, wheelchairs and in-home care. Specialty wheelchairs and case management services are also routinely offered.

In contrast, most commercial insurers hesitate to fully cover in-home care, specialty wheelchairs and other adaptive devices, doctors and patients say.

"HMOs are frequent offenders when it comes to providing rehab," Nieshoff said.

Dr. David Wolf, a Westland obstetrician who was paralyzed from the waist down in a July 29 go-cart accident, said his injury is depleting his finances because his insurance won't cover items considered basic.

Since his injury, he's paid $1,500 for a chair he can use in the shower to avoid taking a sponge bath in his bed, $4,000 for shower alterations and $900 for weights he uses to strengthen his upper body.

"If you're someone who doesn't have any money, what would you do?" Wolf said. "I had no idea about this stuff, no idea people had to go through this. In this game that we're in, standard care should be the same for everybody."

Ruben Lucas, a 31-year-old Westland man who was recently partly paralyzed as a result of a gunshot wound, is in a similar situation with his insurance company.

His initial daily in-patient therapy services have been whittled down to 60 days of out-patient rehabilitation a year. Lucas experienced delays in receiving a wheelchair and his insurance co-payment has increased.

Costly follow-up care

Whether covered by insurance or partly by spinal cord patients themselves, follow-up care is expensive.

Costs can reach $572,000 the first year and hit about $100,000 every year after that, according to the National Spinal Cord Injury Statistical Center in Birmingham, Ala.

"If you have commercial insurance, you have to be fabulously wealthy or completely destitute or you will get the minimal level of service," Nieshoff said.

"It's expensive and insurers, as a matter of financial survival, have decided to cut costs at the expense of this minority group of patients."

Some families are left with no choice except to turn their loved ones over to state-run nursing homes.

"The tragedy lies within the system," said Nieshoff, who is also an assistant professor at Wayne State University's School of Medicine. "When I was injured there was more money in the system but cutbacks have dried up medical services markedly."

Appendix 3

"Doctor Learns to Live as Patient after Ohio Go-Kart Mishap"

Courtesy of *The News-Herald*
Published on Wednesday, August 22, 2001

D r. David Wolf, a prominent Trenton physician, is learning to adjust to life a as paraplegic.

The 54-year-old crashed during a go-kart race at Toledo (Ohio) Speedway on July 29. His injuries left him paralyzed from the waist down.

"I was on the inside of the second row and when we were coming around the first turn, two cars were spinning in front of me," Wolf said Monday from his room in the Rehabilitation Institute of Michigan in Detroit.

To avoid hitting the go-karts, he tried to pass them on the outside of the track. As he did, however, he lost control and smashed into the wall.

Wolf estimated that he was going about 50 mph when his go-kart crashed.

"It was such a force that it drove my engine and disc brake forward," he said.

The disc brake went through his seat and fractured Wolf's lower back. He also fractured eight ribs on his left side and two on the right.

Wolf was taken to St. Vincent's Mercy Medical Center in Toldeo, where he underwent neurosurgery Aug 2.

"There was no hope of me moving my legs again," Wolf said. "But the surgery was a way to stabilize my lower spine so that additional damage wouldn't be done."

He was transferred to the Rehabilitation Institute on Aug. 15.

"I am learning how to get back to normal," he said.

Every day, Wolf goes through occupational and physical therapy regimes, lifts weights and learns how to get around in a wheelchair.

He expects to be in rehabilitation for about two months.

Dealing with the sudden change in his life has proven to be a challenge for the obstetrician/gynecologist.

"As a physician, I was used to being independent," Wolf said. "It's difficult to get used to being a dependent person and being a patient that has to wait for other people to help you. But I think it will make me a better doctor because I'll be more sympathetic to my patients' desires and thoughts because I know what it's like to be in bed and in pain."

Although he probably will no longer deliver babies, Wolf intends to continue doing gynecological surgery and mentor new doctors in the residency program at Riverside Osteopathic Hospital.

He hopes to be back to his Trenton practice and his duties at the hospital in a matter of months.

Appendix 4

"A Heartfelt Thank-You from Dr. David Wolf"

Courtesy of *The News-Herald*
Published on Sunday, September 9, 2001

Dear patients, friends, and colleagues,

I want to thank you from the bottom of my heart for the unbelievable outpouring of support, love and prayers since my accident on July 29, 2001. To the thousands of patients who sent gifts and cards of encouragement, I can only say two things. First, you are the greatest! Second, I will be back in the office providing OB/GYN care for you in the near future.

To my friends and colleagues, you have no idea how much your visits and support have meant to me, Anita, and our children. To take time from your busy schedules, in some cases flying in from around the country, is unbelievable and I will cherish your kindness forever.

It is true that I face new challenges, but the Lord has showered me with countless blessings and I remain the luckiest man alive. With the unbelievable support of my family, friends, patients, and colleagues, I accept and embrace these challenges. The Lord has changed the path of my journey, but my resolve, determination, and goals remain as strong and focused as ever. As the dedication at my office entrance proclaims: "To God and the caring of women and their unborn babies."

Thank you and may God bless each and every one of you!

CPWJfO.o.

David L. Wolf, D.O.

Appendix 5

"Doctor on the Mend:
Faith Defines Recovery for David Wolf"

Story by Pat Andrews, Courtesy of *The News-Herald*
Published on Wednesday, January 30, 2002

When bad things happen to good people, it can test the faith of all of us.

What possible reason could there be that David Wolf, described over and over by patients and friends as one of the most caring of physicians, would suddenly have his working world as he knew it come to a sudden and shocking end in July on a go-kart track in Ohio?

It took but a split second last summer to take Wolf, a prominent obstetrics/gynecology specialist who has delivered more than 10,000 babies, to be in a desperate fight for his own life.

The question, "Why him? Why Dr. Wolf?" was echoed from his birthplace in Indiana to his practice in Trenton and back down to Toledo.

Surprisingly, he blames no one but himself.

The accident that rendered him

a paraplegic, unable to move from the waist down, was, in a way, fate. He is the first to say it was the result of his passion for a sport he enjoyed in his youth and took up again two years ago at the age of 52, over the strong objection of Anita, his wife of 30 years.

"I've always been adrenaline-charged and when I decide to do something, it is fully and completely," he said.

Wolf said that a friend, Danny Doyle, was the instigator in getting him back in a racing mode—something he had not done for nearly 40 years.

"My wife was not for it, not in the least," Wolf said, jokingly. "I found ways, speaking engagements and lectures to pay for my hobby so she would allow me to play.

"The very first year I was semi-successful, but I wanted more, naturally. I bought my own kart, got a first-class paint job, and the next year I was leading the division almost to the end.

"Now, you must realize that I was 53 at the time and the average age of the drivers was around 25."

Wolf might have captured the top trophy prize in his division that year had it not been for a family crisis. His mother, living in another state, required emergency surgery and he flew to be with her rather than on the track.

When the 2001 season rolled around, Wolf had added two seasoned mechanics to his team and he was going for gold.

The July 29 race was a test of sorts for a more grueling 500-mile endurance race later in the season. No points were involved—it was strictly for practice.

Wolf was, quite frankly, the leader of the pack.

"I never once went out on a track to lose," he said. "I always wanted to be No. 1. But I also knew the dangers."

That particular race on asphalt was in an alcohol-powered kart, rather than gasoline-fueled—the same format expected for the 500-mile race.

"I remember being third back when the two drivers in front of me began spinning," he said. "I had to make a quick and critical decision.

"Going an estimated 70 miles per hour, my only chance was to go to the outside of the cars. I hit the cement retainer wall.

"As I look back at it now, I feel that if I had not taken that course, I probably would have killed one or both of the other drivers, or severely injured them."

Wolf's back was broken when the brake rotor behind him punctured his seat. He also suffered extensive spinal cord injuries and broke eight ribs.

Track officials instantly went into action and the ambulance on site transported the doctor within a matter of minutes to the emergency room at nearby St. Vincent Mercy Medical Center in Toledo.

Wolf's wife was spending the afternoon at home and received a call that her husband had been injured and taken to the hospital. Because their son, Brad, 20, was using one of the family cars, she suddenly found herself without transportation from their residence in Trenton.

A family friend, Dr. Robert Sauter, was called. He drove Anita Wolf to Toledo.

Wolf said his wife was unprepared for what she was told.

"I'm thankful every day that Bob was with her," he said. "She imagined that I had a broken bone or two."

Brad Wolf arrived a few hours later, as did the couple's daughter, Raquel, 23.

"I'm told that my daughter fainted at the news and my son just beat at a wall," Wolf said. "They were filled with such emotion at what had happened to their father. I cannot imagine the pain I caused them."

The physician was on a respirator and his lungs were filling with blood. It was two days before surgeons were able to put their skills to the test to begin to repair their colleague.

A six-hour surgery placed a titanium rod from his shoulders to his waist.

When word of the accident reached patients—current and former—the phone calls and letters began flooding the family home and the office.

Wolf estimated that he received more than 1,500 expressions of cheer.

"How do you thank that many people?" he asked.

The doctors at St. Vincent determined that Wolf could be released after a two-week stay. But the facility had been his comfort zone, where his needs were taken care of by staff, not family.

Now, he had to face a new challenge.

"I knew that I had the courage to press on and I did," he said. "I chose the Rehabilitation Institute of Michigan in Detroit for what would be four weeks of intensive training."

One of the main reasons Wolf selected that facility was the reputation of one of its staff members.

"Another physician—Dr. Edward Nieshoff—is a quadriplegic," Wolf said. "Not only could he relate to me and answer more personal questions that I had, he demonstrated a symbol that there is hope."

Each day brings a new experience and a new facet to Wolf's life. It takes him more than 2½ hours to get up from his bed, shower and shave.

"I was the ultimate workaholic, putting in days that extended well past midnight in an effort to see patients and give them my full attention," he said.

"I can remember one instance where I almost missed an early morning surgery that my daughter was having on her knee. I had completely worked through the night. At that point, my staff and my wife said the after-midnight hours had to stop except in an emergency."

Wolf said he always has been the type of person who is adrenaline-driven and requires little sleep, sometimes less than four hours a night.

"That has all changed," he said. "Everything is an effort, but I feel there are reasons for everything, and mentally I want to be the positive person I was before the accident."

Wolf returned Jan. 14 to a practice he shares with two other physicians, just blocks from Riverside Osteopathic Hospital.

He saw eight patients that day—all current—and it brought him great satisfaction.

"Yes, I already miss the exuberant feeling one gets when a delivery is imminent, and I used to race down the alley behind the building to get to the hospital," he said.

Wolf has made a decision not to take a paycheck from the practice.

"I have disability insurance and I don't feel that it is fair to my fellow doctors at this point," he said.

Whether or not there will be new patients in Wolf's future is an unknown. He said that when an individual calls the office, the staff explains his limitations.

That possibly is the only thing that has brought a touch of sadness to the doctor. He readily admits to being patient-motivated and to providing the ultimate in care.

Other than that, his family and friends say, he has been the strong one throughout the last six months.

Wolf, who grew up in Kokomo, Ind., and did his undergraduate work at Manchester College and Indiana University, said he has always been a religious person.

When his present office was constructed the plan included a chapel in the basement area and a plaque at the entryway that dedicated the structure to the unborn child.

It is that personal faith that not only has given him the will to go on, but also has supported his family, friends and staff.

Just recently he completed a driver's training course at the Rehabilitation Center.

"The instructor said it would take five complete days of class time to become certified," he said. "The old competitive feeling in me kicked in, and on the first day, I had aced the hospital parking lot and had persuaded my instructor to let me go up and down the main streets. By day two, I was going up and down the expressway.

"She just couldn't believe that anyone could learn the hand/brake coordination process that quickly. But I was determined."

A specially fitted van on order will allow Wolf more mobility in his life. He must, however, use a very rigid wheelchair, and he is searching for ways to be able to use the vehicle and be able to get that chair or another model in and out by himself.

A one-level condominium has been purchased and the bathroom and garage have been modified for his needs.

The Wolf family has a condo near a northern Michigan ski resort and that, too, has been made barrier-free and a shower installed that will allow him easy access.

"We are still working on our lake home in Indiana," he said. "You just don't realize how costly these changes are, and I feel very lucky that I have been able to afford what I need."

Wolf must watch his weight, especially in the midsection where he has no feeling.

He has taken a liking to Slim Fast and he works with a personal trainer several hours each week.

Skip Bunton at Body Specs in Wyandotte has trained many Olympic athletes during his 20-year-plus career.

"I see that intensity to succeed in Dr. Wolf," Bunton said.

Bunton works with the doctor for an hour three times a week and said the most difficult part has been preparing his client physiologically for what was going to be a new lifestyle.

"He didn't know what to expect or the strength it would take to be what he expected of himself," Bunton added. "He is one amazing man."

Wolf also believes that he has a positive message to convey to others. One that attests to his belief in God no matter what occurs in one's life.

He has spoken several times at a local church and found the audience to be very receptive.

"If the minister goes on for more than an hour, people seem to grumble," he said, laughing. "I've had people stay to listen for more than 90 minutes."

The world is not barrier-free, as Wolf has learned. He is making do, but wants to be part of changes.

"I've been getting my hair cut for years and years at the same place in Wyandotte," he said. "After the accident, I discovered there were no curb cuts. The handicapped parking was at the rear and you had to bang on the back door."

On a recent Sunday, Wolf and his wife went out for lunch after church services.

"It was fine and the manager found a spot that my wheelchair could maneuver," he said.

"When we were ready to leave, I think that 10 people had to get up and move their chairs so I could get out. For a moment, I was embarrassed ... but I knew that it was just a test of faith. I think I passed."

Sport is for all ages

What used to be a fun sport for youngsters has become a high-tech competition for adults. The world of go-karting has taken off across the country and novice drivers are sharing the pits with almost pros.

The small one-seater vehicles can cost several hundred to several thousand dollars and are designed to attain speeds of 55 to 75 mph. Briggs and Stratton and Yahama are two popular manufacturers.

The Premiere Karting Association hosts weekly asphalt oval kart races on Sundays at Toledo Speedway in Ohio. Drivers, as well as spectators, are welcome.

World Karting Association rules and regulations are used in the races.

Described as safe, competitive, wheel-to-wheel racing, it is an enjoyable sport for a growing audience.

An accident in July involving Dr. David Wolf of Trenton has ensured that even more rules of safety are enforced.

Later in the year, Greer Racing Karts & Parts of Luna Pier began to market a new safety device to prevent the brake rotor from becoming detached and ramming the driver's seat.

Wolf was paralyzed from the waist down after the brake rotor from his kart punctured the seat, injuring his spinal cord.

The simple part developed by Green Racing Karts retails for $14.95 plus shipping and the designers are donating 50 cents from each sale to spinal cord research.

The designers, Scott Nuss and Roy Arblaster, have named the brake rotor protector "The Wolf Plate."

Notes

1. Bruce H. Wilkinson, *The Prayer of Jabez* (Sisters, Oregon: Multnomah Publishers, Inc., 2000).

2. Oswald Chambers, *My Utmost for His Highest* (Grand Rapids, Michigan: Discovery House Publishers, 1992), message for August 11.

3. *Press On* (aka *En Cristo Yo Vencere*), words and music by Dan Burgess, © 1983 Belwin-Mills Publishing Corp. All rights administered by Alfred Publishing Co., Inc. All rights reserved. Used by permission of Alfred Music.

4. *It Is Well with My Soul*, words by Horatio G. Spafford, 1873, music by Philip P. Bliss, Gospel Hymns No. 2, by P. P. Bliss and Ira. D. Sankey (New York: Biglow & Main, 1876), number 76. Public domain.

5. Stephen R. Covey, *The 7 Habits of Highly Effective People* (New York, New York: Simon and Schuster, 1989).

6. Charles Swindoll, *Paul: A Man of Grace and Grit* (Nashville, TN: Thomas Nelson, 2002).

7. Loren Eisley, *The Star Thrower* (New York, NY: Times Books, First Harvest edition, 1979), 171–173.

8. James Dobson, *Stories of the Heart and Home* (Nashville, Tenn.: Word Publishing, 2000). 127.

9. George Bernard Shaw, speech given at the Municipal Technical College and School of Art in Brighton (1907).

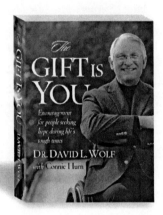

Copies of this book may be
purchased online at

www.amazon.com and
www.xulonpress.com/bookstore

୫୬

To schedule a presentation by Dr. Wolf or
to provide comments about *The Gift Is You,*
go to
www.TheGiftIsYou.org

CPSIA information can be obtained at www.ICGtesting.com
Printed in the USA
BVOW05s1736140814

362725BV00003B/607/P